ADVENTURES IN SOLITUDE

Books By

DAVID GRAYSON

Adventures in Solitude

Adventures in Contentment

Adventures in Friendship

Adventures in Understanding

A Day of Pleasant Bread

Great Possessions

The Friendly Road

The Countryman's Year

Under My Elm

*Welcome to the fellowship of readers who enjoy fine literature from the country. We invite you to write or call for our free monthly publication **The Grayson Letter**, which offers thoughts, observations and quotations from fine books promoting a peaceful lifestyle.*

RENAISSANCE HOUSE PUBLISHERS

541 Oak ~ PO Box 177 ~ Frederick, CO 80530

Call toll free **1-800-521-9221**

ADVENTURES
IN SOLITUDE

By
DAVID GRAYSON

Illustrated By
D<small>AVID</small> H<small>ENDRICKSON</small>

RENAISSANCE HOUSE
PUBLISHERS

ISBN: 1-55838-111-2

RENAISSANCE HOUSE PUBLISHERS
A Division of Jende-Hagan, Inc.
541 Oak Street ~ P.O. Box 177
Frederick, CO   80530
1-800-521-9221

Cover illustration from North Wind Picture Archives

Library of Congress Cataloging in Publication
Grayson, David, 1870-1946.
    Adventures in solitude / by David Grayson ; illustrated
by David Hendrickson.
        p.   cm.
    Reprint. Originally published: New York : Doubleday,
Doran, c1931.
    ISBN 1-55838-111-2 : $13.95
    1. Grayson, David, 1870-1946--Biography--Health.
2. Authors,   American--20th century--Biography.
3. Solitude.   I. Title.
PS3503.A5448Z467   1990
818'.5403--dc20
[B]   90-30042
                                                              CIP

TO
MY FRIEND
John S. Phillips

FOREWORD

SOLITUDE is not the exceptional state of man: it is the normal. Every man spends most of his time alone with himself: how much more in periods of illness or of sorrow. A whole world, invisible without, a man creates within his own personality. There he lives; there he adventures; there he is happy, if he is happy; there he suffers. If he cannot command this world of his own making he is miserable indeed.

This little book deals with a fortunate, if enforced, solitude, and the effort of a man to make or find his own felicity.

CONTENTS

I ILLNESS

I

ILLNESS

". . . Prisoner, tell me who was it that wrought this unbreakable chain?"

"It was I," said the prisoner, "who forged this chain very carefully."

TAGORE: *"Gitanjali."*

WEEKS I lay there. When I first lay down in that little room the sun was setting every evening well to the northward of the spire I could see from my window, far across rolling hills, laden then with the gorgeous foliage of autumn. I saw it creep daily southward. In illness one treasures the minutest details of the changing day. An evening came—I had feared lest it be cloudy—when the slim spire, at sunset, pierced the golden globe itself, and the buttressed shoulders of the church stood out dark and sharp against a burning background, a picture unforgettably etched in gold. After that, day by day, the sun set among hills that grew barren and drearier, among trees that had shed their autumn glory, and presently held up to the sky the gaunt tracery of approaching winter.

Illness, like its elder brother, death, is a cessation. Life stops. Identity blurs. One hangs up his personality with his clothes in the closet and becomes a case—the patient in No. 12. No longer quite a man, but a condition, a problem, stretched out there for daily examination, looked down upon, peered into, charted on paper with graphs like the rise and fall in the price of wheat. It is this indignity even more than the pain and the weakness and the boredom that makes the experience, for a man with any imagination, difficult to bear. To be something, and then to be nothing! It is no doubt one of the commonest of human experiences—since I myself have known it, it seems as though all the world had been ill—and yet no one can ever know, for himself, until it has come to him, what it means to be set aside, lifted arrogantly out of his active labour, and put down hori-

zontal and helpless in bed. With whisperers
tiptoeing about, queer distant clocks striking
the hours through the long night, the weary
reiteration of the processes of medication, a hot
and restless pillow. Everything minutely
ordered, taken ruthlessly out of one's own
habitual and accustomed hands—what to eat,
what to drink, when to sleep, when to sit up,
when to turn over—sad business! Even though
one may have the assurances of those who
should know, that he will ultimately recover,
yet it seems somehow, in the beginning at least,
that everything is lost. What value have such
easy and optimistic prophecies? Does anyone
know? Does anyone ever tell the truth to a man
in bed?

All my life, except for a time in my youth, I
had had robust health, and the kind of contentment that goes with it. Minor disabilities, a
day or so here, a week there, though sometimes
irritating, had never shaken an underlying and
abiding sense of well-being. To-morrow I shall
be well again! Such interruptions were even to
be cherished: one could go to bed with a book.

Having health a man can enjoy everything,

. . . the mere fact, consciousness—these forms—the
    power of motion,
The least insect or animal—the senses—eyesight—
    love.

I had never known what it meant to be too
weary to look up to the hills at evening for a
sure benediction, or to find, in the shorn
meadows, peace. As to safety, the desire of the
fragile and the vulnerable, I had never even
paused to consider it. I had within me, however deeply hidden, "a certain jollity of mind,
pickled in the scorn of fortune." I did whatever offered itself strongly to my taste, sometimes adventuring in the country where I have
lived so many years—it is beautiful enough,
most of the time, for gods to dwell in—and
sometimes employing myself in grubbing labour
that brought me friends I liked or money I
needed. It seems to me now, as I look back, that
I wanted nothing I did not have. I enjoyed a
kind of busy contentment of oblivion, like that
of a child, of which, when one asked me seri-

ously: "Will it endure through the hard time coming?" I made believe I did not hear, glanced at the long shadows that lay across my garden, and turned another page in the labour of the day. What did it matter? I was content.

Life is a process which gradually jolts our self-sufficiency into understanding—possibly even serenity—if we can endure long enough to complete the process.

How well I remember now the onset of my illness. At first sly hints and warnings, to which I paid slight attention. I waked up heavy and weary instead of bounding out of bed. Twinges! Burning in the eyes and behind the eyes. There were mornings when I had no joy in what I saw, nor cared for what I heard. At first I kept quiet and made a joke of it—only weaklings went to doctors! There were moments of anger; moments of surprise; moments of downright fear. I had somehow offended nature, and would make my offering in humility, praying that the fire might descend and the earth smile again.

On the day that I went away from home I remember vividly Harriet standing there in the doorway. We are Northern, our race is Northern; we do not easily express all we feel. But I knew! I knew something of what she felt by the curve at the corner of her lips and the curious withdrawn expression in her eyes. When we are well we take so much for granted. This too, this painful parting, was an uncalculated element of a new experience. One is singled out for suffering. He goes alone; he takes no one with him.

I remember the dismal railroad journey, noisy, close, hot. Now that the mind had surrendered—it was not all a joke!—it seemed impossible to keep from thinking of each different symptom, wondering, calculating, dreading. Health is self-forgetfulness: to be ill is to be self-centred. One's mind is like a burning glass: it can literally blister any part of the body by the intensity of its concentration.

Eight doctors there were with their "diagnostic indications," and beyond them, a foreordained and predestined terror, awaited the surgeon. I found the examination itself difficult to endure. It was humiliatingly familiar, a challenge to one's dignity and personality: something positively obscene. I knew better, at a later time, the understanding, yes, and the sympathy, that lay back of those painful probings; but at the moment it was hard to bear. It seemed somehow the end of everything! I remember trying to find some comfort in two lines of a bitter philosophy of resignation that clung dimly to my mind:

We have lived, we have loved, we have suffered . . . even so.
Shall we not take the ebb who had the flow?

Worst of all I dreaded the uncertainty. How ignorant, after all, we are of ourselves that we must await the decision of strangers to know whether we are to live or die. Would it be two weeks, or four, or eight? Who could tell? One's whens elicit only ifs. I was to rest under observation in a quiet small hospital until the doctors made sure of what to do; after that I

was to go to the great hospital and the surgeon.
I had revelled in times past in well ordered certainties. To-morrow morning I would work at
such and such a task; at noon meet my friend
Darrow; at three drive to town with many
errands to do; at five perhaps a tramp by the
back road to North Hadley—but this was a
place where one could have no certainties of his
own whatsoever: no decisions; nothing. In the
meantime—quiet! Not the teeming quiet I love,
of country roads with friendly people going by,
or the thoughtful quiet of my own garden, or
the beautiful quiet of the still banks of hill
streams in Pelham or Shutesbury—but in-
anition of body that whetted without satisfying the appetite of the mind. Quiet. No visitors, no letters, no books (at first)—nothing!
Vacuity. To one who loved life!

In the beginning I thought I could not bear
it. I would get up in broad daylight, put on my
clothes, lift up my head, and walk out. Anything was better than this. A man, even in illness, is a free agent, is he not? It is his own
life he is risking? How could one lie watching

forever the angle of light that came through
the half-open door? How listen with straining
ears to sounds of distant pain or lonely weariness? How pretend to a hopefulness one could
not feel? It was all wrong. They could ensure,
indeed, quiet for the body, but what man among
them all possessed the genius to "still the beating mind"? Who could minister to that part of
me—the hot core of me—they did not find in-
dicated after the last X-ray plate had been
taken; which even the cunning pathologist, with
his delicate instruments, laying me apart after
I am dead, will not discover?

Yes, this was the end. This was the irre-
trievable experience. Strange it should come in
this way.

II THE LITTLE ROOM

II

THE LITTLE ROOM

*A man of understanding hath lost nothing,
if he yet have himselfe.*

I DID not get up and walk out. I could not.
But I was nevertheless in hot revolt. I
hated this abnormal concentration upon the ills
and defects of human life, my own and others'.
It offended every hard-won principle of my
life. I hated the atmosphere of studied cheer-
fulness—the doctor marching in of a morning, a flower in his buttonhole, his face glowing
ruddily after a walk in the crisp autumn air,
his ready joke, his jaunty laughter! Oh, I
played up to him, but I was secretly and bit-
terly envious—I who loved nothing in this
world better than a tramp on a glorious morning. At the same time I hated myself for the

15

puerility of my envy. And the nurses, also glowing with health—offensively glowing—bustling, cheerful—that starched tyranny! I had afterwards a different view of nurses—one of them could whistle like a starling—but in those early days, in cheerfully condemning me to helplessness, they incited me to revolt, to skepticism, to pessimism.

"This," said I to myself, "is not a man's world at all. It is a kind of matriarchy!"

This led me to think, not without a kind of humour, of a queer old book among my treasures, published not long after Shakespeare's death, called "The Feminine Monarchie"—a treatise on honeybees, "shewing Their Admirable Nature and Properties, together with the Right Ordering of them from time to time." It bore a flattering dedication, I remembered, to Queen Elizabeth.

Well, this was truly a "feminine monarchie" I lived in. Except for the distant, glowing, planetary doctor, one's day was dominated from early morning until late at night by feminine autocrats. Dominated to embarrassment. A

man, I maintain, does not easily submit to the
indignity of being told when his hair is to be
brushed, his face washed, his pajamas changed!

"If ever I escape from this tyranny," I said
to myself, "I will consider writing a new Feminine Monarchie, and do it, as old Charles But-
ler did it, 'out of experience.'"

So I began studying, not without some sly
amusement, which I sternly repressed, their
Admirable Nature and Properties, though I
have never dared to write down my observations, since I could not be sure, even after
months of experience, that I understood "the
right ordering of them from time to time."

Miserable days they were, those earlier ones,
far more difficult to bear than the pain, the
weakness, even the sleepless or opiated nights
that came later in the great hospital. For
misery, after all, is not physical—pain can be
borne, helplessness somehow endured—misery
is always mental. Tragedy is mental. It is what
we think, not what we suffer, that destroys us.
It is the disturbance of ordered life, the sense

of inadequacy, the conviction of failure that crush the soul. All men, ill or well, lead frustrated lives, all of us fall short of our hopes and ideals. Human strength is never enough to meet problems and difficulties that are infinite. Human life is never long enough! We suffer because we are finite among infinite realities; because the universe is too great for us.

Yes, we are all alike: we all fail. The difference between men lies in the way they face disaster, meet the tragic facts of their existence. That man is successful who has learned to live triumphantly within his limitations. I had not only never met the real problem adequately—I can see it now—I had never even faced it squarely until I reached the experience which I am here describing, when everything I loved, all I hoped for, seemed suddenly snatched away from me.

In the long hours of night when I could not sleep—sleep is often the denied anodyne of suffering—I drove my mind in a weary round of self-recrimination, probing the causes of my downfall, seeking some other than myself to blame, some chance incident of five or ten or twenty years ago that might if—and if—and if. And always I came out of these weary excursions exactly where I went in, with a sense of utter futility and failure. I destroyed the present, of which I was sure, with remorse for the past, which I could not change, and apprehension of the future, which I might never know.

I think of those days now with wonder and with shame.

This mood of utter wretchedness continued for many days. One night, as I lay quite still but intolerably awake in my half-darkened room, I heard the sound of a man sighing, or groaning, as though his very soul were in torment. I began to listen with a hushed intensity of interest. There it was again! What weariness, pain, hopeless longing! I knew nothing whatever about the patient next door—I had been too much wrapped up in my own misery even to inquire. I had heard from time to time the rumble of his voice through the wall, and occasionally a word or two as of someone speaking at his door. It came to me now with a strange sense of discovery that this was a human being, a person, suffering as I was, possibly far worse than I was. No doubt he had left friends and work and comfort he prized as much as I did. No doubt the future looked black also to him. My mind at once began conjecturing, a thousand ways, the unknown life and problems of the man lying there so close to me, yet entirely unknown. What was he like, where was he from, what was the train of events that had brought him, also, to this sad place? For a moment, in the sharpness of my interest, my strained listening, I forgot my own illness.

There it was again: the weary sighing, a few low words that sounded like a melancholy prayer. I cannot tell how deeply it affected me. At the very moment when I was beginning to realize that I was not the only sufferer in the world, that here was a man who might be even more sadly afflicted than I, it came to me with inexpressible power and poignancy that both of us, lying there side by side, unknown to each other, were as nothing compared with the hundreds, the thousands, of men and women in the hospitals of that great city, each with his own burden of suffering, each turning and twisting in the maze of his own discomforting thoughts. What a stupendous weight of illness, weakness, suffering, misery, in an entire state!

I am trying to put down these thoughts just as they came upon me, tumultuously, in the dark intensity of that night. It may be that my own straining weakness accounted in part for the extraordinary sharpness and force of the impression I had: it was what I felt. I had known before, certainly, that there was an immense burden of illness and suffering in the world, but I had known it only as knowledge, not as experience, not as *feeling*. Sometimes in the past, when friends had been ill or sad or discouraged, I, from my haven of security, had been able to help them—or thought I helped—with assurances of strength or courage. But here was the stark reality! I was myself a part of an inconceivable sink of human misery: I could help no one else; no one could help me.

For a day or so my mind struggled fever-
ishly, if fruitlessly, with these new thoughts of
the universality of human suffering. In one
way I found my own situation somewhat re-
lieved. There was a kind of comfort and satisfaction—yes, satisfaction—in knowing that I
was no worse than hundreds of other men and
women; and I had also a curious and recurrent
sense of a new understanding, an entirely new
relationship, between human beings, not one
based upon common enjoyment, but upon common misery. These new thoughts, however,
proved no permanent abatement of my own ills.
After a day or so they seemed even to increase
my weariness and hopelessness. My own
chances, the chances of any individual in such
a chaos of suffering, seemed even less en-
couraging. I was not an exception: I was the
rule. I thought of all the vast paraphernalia of
hospitals, medical faculties, highly trained
physicians and nurses, and how impotent they
were to cope with the appalling human disability
that afflicted the world.

Misery may love company, but company does not cure misery. In illness one is, after all, terribly alone.

I will not enlarge further upon the wretchedness of those unhappy days. One morning, some two weeks after I lay down in that bed, I had a curious and deep inner experience. I do not know what caused it, save that I seem to have explored every other passage in the mazes of a weary mind, but suddenly I roused up and turned fiercely upon myself:

"What a ridiculous creature you are," I said, "bowled over with scarcely a struggle by one of the oldest, commonest, simplest difficulties that beset human beings. Even your inner fortress taken!"

Had I, then, lived a busy life for so many years, had I made good friends, had I visited strange and interesting places, had I read many books with delight—and out of all these overflowing experiences, a life's entire accumulation, was there nothing left to carry me through a few weeks or even months in bed? Had I in reality been wholly dependent upon the external interests which had filled my hours? Had I come to such a pass that I had no resources of the spirit? Was I on such terms with myself, after long and close association, that it was hopeless misery to live alone with myself?

I cannot tell with what burning urgency these questions assailed me. Though I did not stir in my bed, nor break the calm monotony with which my nurse, sitting there by the window, stitched at the bit of fancy work she held in her hand, my mind was in the fiercest turmoil. It seemed to me that I had come to the crucial test of my whole life—and at a time when I was, because of my physical weakness, least able to bear it.

The nurse, looking at me, the outer shell of me, shook her head dubiously.

"You have something on your mind," said she, examining the thermometer she had taken from between my lips.

I said nothing.

"You are disturbed," said she.

"Yes," said I, "I am disturbed. It is time that I was disturbed."

"You must be quiet," said she. "Everything depends upon your being quiet."

"Quiet," said I, "is what I most desire."

An immense weariness came down upon me. I could not think longer or with clarity. I had been stripped bare; I had no defenses left. I felt as though my life had amounted to nothing whatsoever: opinions and beliefs upon which I had rested with oblivious content furnished no refuge in the storm. For it so often happens that when a man has reached the point where he feels that he is beginning to know how to command his life and the tools of his employment, to reap the harvest of his labour, tragedy of one sort or another touches him on the shoulder.

"Can you bear it?" Or, if he winces, "Where now is your vaunted philosophy?"

When the mind is deeply stirred it seems to go on with its work in its own subterranean caverns, even when the physical husk of the body is unconscious with suffering or with sleep. Hours later, in the night, when I awakened, the tumultuous thoughts of the previous day, returning powerfully, presented an entirely new aspect of my situation—one that had not occurred to me before. While it was true that everything that had constituted a pleasant and satisfying life for me—my robust physical health, my habitual and interesting work, and all my books, my letters, my friends—while all these had been stripped away, I was still possessed of my own mind and my own thoughts. I had, after all, my own inner life. I had my life!

In the telling, in cold words, this may seem no remarkable conclusion, still less a discovery. Of course! It was axiomatic: a child would know as much. But to me, lying there in bed, restless and miserable, it came with a wave of feeling that flooded my whole being. It was true: I had in reality, however helpless, vast inner possessions upon which I had not counted. Of all that I really was I had so much left!

A couplet that had long lain concealed in my memory came to me with fresh significance:

> Still to ourselves in every place consigned
> Our own felicity we make or find.

It was true—it was true! I was consigned to myself here in this gabled room—after the manner of all prisoners, all sick men, all those fortunately banished or outcast. I was condemned to enforced quiet, to an utter vacuity of outward possessions and ordinary interests. I was consigned to myself: and no one but myself could make or find my felicity. No doctor, however cunning, no nurse, however skilful; no prophet, or preacher, or book; not riches; not friends: it was only this strange something that was within me that could find me peace or comfort.

Yes, words are poor things: they express inadequately the power and the beauty of thoughts which shake or mould our lives.

This was the beginning: it is with the tests and explorations of this idea, coming so power-

fully into my mind, that I shall now write, bas-
ing what I have to say upon notes that I soon
began to scrawl, a few a day, as I was able, in
a little book I kept in the drawer of the desk
that stood near the head of my bed.

III   THE QUIET COUNTRY OF THE MIND

III

THE QUIET COUNTRY OF THE MIND

He most doth dwell in bliss
That hath a quiet mind.

MY ROOM was in the top of the house, not large, large enough. Part of the ceiling was cut away by the roof, but there was a fine gable window opening to the west where I could see, looking along the white ridge of the counterpane, which was *me,* the hills and the distant spire of which I have already spoken. At my right, only a few feet distant, if I turned my head, I could see through the other window the fretwork branches of a lordly beech tree, upon which still clung a remnant of the painted foliage of autumn. They reached so close that I could have leaned out—if I could have leaned out!—and touched fingers with them. Each morning, about sunrise—time meant nothing to one in my case—two or three starlings came to sit on the branches of the beech. They began talking to one another quite intimately, in their own language, which at that time I did not understand, much less care to hear.

I did not like starlings.

I did not like to have reminders of the free world I could not enjoy.

"Quiet," I had said to the nurse, "is what I most desire."

I had said it somewhat ironically. For years I had been secretly longing for quiet, for retirement, for a chance to think—or I said I had. I had thought of the joy of "going into the silence" described by the old religionists, where one could "lift off thought after thought, passion after passion," until one reached the inmost depth of all. Well, I now had my desires involuntarily fulfilled: here in this high gabled room both quiet and retirement, such as they were, had been conferred upon me, and I was not content. It was not an easy matter, even after I had discovered the true secret and place of my possessions, that they were inward, to enter upon their enjoyment or use them as a sure way to tranquillity. I know I stumbled horribly, slipping back again and again to the weary suffering, the self-recrimination, of the early days of my imprisonment.

My first deliberate effort to get at my hoarded possessions and thus turn my mind away from the misery of my situation, was prompted, I think, by the extraordinary power with which the couplet I have already repeated—"Still to ourselves in every place consigned"—had come back to me. It had been like the precipitate which the chemist pours into a cloudy mixture to make it suddenly clear. It had convinced me that I and none other was the architect of my felicity. This set me to wondering if there were not other life-saving passages tucked away in my memory: and I began at once to try to recapture old poetry, even old prose, that I had committed to memory in my youth and thought I had forgotten. At first, like a lost sailor in a heavy sea, I seized upon any chance spar—a line of any old poem or ballad, any flotsam of prose cast up by a driven memory, and found it surprising, once I had fixed my mind upon it, how I could recover entire stanzas, even whole poems that I had not thought about for many years. In my boyhood I memorized easily—a gift which, I am sad to say, has left me—especially galloping or romantic verse like "The Lady of the Lake," "The Prisoner of Chillon," Bürger's "Ballad of William and Helen," and Tennyson's "Locksley Hall." I loved the sonorous roll of "Thanatopsis," and the splendid imagery in passages from Isaiah, Ecclesiastes, and the Psalms which, though I was constrained to learn them, often gave me a strange thrill of pleasure.

In the long hours of night when I could not sleep, I now began to reclaim these lost treasures, catching up a phrase here, a rhyme or rhythm there, and piecing them together with an increasing delight that ate up the weary hours. Time was nothing to me. I must have worked several days trying to recapture cer-

tain of William Blake's lines which I have long
loved for their wild ecstasy of beauty. The
third stanza came to me first:

> Bring me my Bow of burning gold
> Bring me my Arrows of desire
> Bring me my Spear! O clouds, unfold!
> Bring me my Chariot of fire.

To a man in my situation there was something challenging, something incalculably in-
spiriting, in these bold words.

> I will not cease from Mental Fight,
> Nor shall my Sword sleep in my hand,
> Till we have built Jerusalem
> In England's green and pleasant land.

How these lines rolled under my tongue as I
lay there silent, in my bed, a trumpet of new
courage, fashioned in beauty. So it was also
that I found comfort in repeating the 38th chapter of Job:

> Who is this that darkeneth counsel by words with-
> out knowledge? . . .
> Canst thou bind the sweet influences of Pleiades, or
> loose the bands of Orion?
> Canst thou bring forth Mazzaroth in his season? or
> canst thou guide Arcturus with his sons?

I recalled also the 12th of Ecclesiastes, the one beginning "Remember now thy Creator," as fine a poem as there is in the language.

This eager pursuit of stored treasure continued for some time, easing my weariness, occupying my mind, giving me, indeed, a kind of satisfaction entirely apart from the content of the lines remembered, for it was a delight in itself to recover out of the mustiness of things forgotten, thoughts, impressions, beauties, that had once interested or thrilled me. I found that I could have my triumphs even as I lay in bed, silent, with the curious tiptoeing life of the hospital flowing around me; and I had a sense that I was somehow getting the better of doctors and nurses who, with all their daily tests, their elaborate records, never once probed the real secret of my life, what I had going on deep down within me—the struggles there, the voyages of discovery, the rich treasures I was now finding in forgotten caverns. While I was often too ill and weary to carry even this engaging occupation as far as I should have liked—there were moments when no effort of mine could lift me

out of the slough of despond—still I had begun
to find a place of comfort in a weary land.

Soon I found myself thinking of the books I
had read, especially those of my early years. I
tried to follow them through, and by recalling
the names of characters and places, strove to
make the incidents live again. I made an especial
effort to see if I could remember with any ex-
actness lines or passages that had impressed
me. So it was that my mind went back to *Gulli-
ver's Travels, Don Quixote, Ivanhoe,* and
others of Scott's novels; *David Copperfield,
Pilgrim's Progress,* and many not so well
known. It was astonishing to me, after a certain
amount of success with the poems, how little
beyond an atmosphere, a general impression, remained to me out of most of these books. Certain characters and incidents in each of them
were, indeed, vivid enough—quite as much alive
as many of the characters and incidents of my
own early life—and there were bits of observation or philosophy which could not be forgotten, like the lines from *Moby Dick*—"From
without no wonderful effect is wrought within

ourselves, unless some interior responding wonder meets it"—but a great part even of the
books I liked best had entirely disappeared. And
that, I have found in recent years, especially
during the later period of my illness, is one of
the reasons why one likes to reread old books:
it is like visiting places once familiar; meeting
friends once well known but half forgotten.
What we remember best, it seems, are those
moments caught by the true poet in times of
high emotion and expressed in words that are
immortal because inevitable. A line of poetry
will stick in a man's mind like a burr.

Of all this effort to recall the books I had
read I soon grew weary: it was, after all, a
kind of game, far less interesting than the
poetry which had often in itself been inspirit-
ing. It was only an anodyne: what I wanted
was a cure. It took my attention away tem-
porarily from the discomforts of the day: it
did not fill my mind with such thoughts as I
"need only regard attentively to be at perfect
ease."

IV FRUITS OF SOLITUDE

IV

FRUITS OF SOLITUDE

. . . then wilt thou not be loth
To leave this Paradise, but shalt possess
A Paradise within thee, happier far.

IT WAS from trying to recreate in some
orderly manner the old, great, childish story
of *Pilgrim's Progress* with the doings of Christian and Hopeful and that delightful dragon of
my boyhood, Apollyon, that I suddenly began
to think of the experiences of John Bunyan himself. He, too, was imprisoned; it was in Bedford
Gaol that he began to delight himself with the
story that has come down through the years.
He turned, not without an apology, from the
tracts and sermons he had written so voluminously, and profiting by his solitude, looked into
his own spirit, sought out his own felicity. He
says of his book—though at that time I could

recover only the substance, not the exact wording, of his apology:

> I only thought to make
> I knew not what: nor did I undertake
> Thereby to please my neighbour; no, not I;
> I did it my own self to gratify.

There is evidence that the staid old puritan had the gravest doubts, because his work really gave him happiness, whether or not he should print the chapters he had written. Was it right to use "feigned words" or to speak in allegories and metaphors when his communication should be "yea, yea" and "nay, nay"?

But he was probably happier in Bedford Gaol, alone with himself, despite the discomforts, the weariness, the constraint—what, indeed, must a jail of the sixteen hundreds have been!—than he ever was before in his life. For he was sojourning in the quiet country of his own mind.

These meditations led me to recall other men of the past who had profited by solitude. I thought of the famous portrait of Robert Louis

Stevenson, propped up in bed—you will remember—with the counterpane drawn up over his shrunken knees, playing the flute. I liked to think of that picture. He was not only ill, but banished from old scenes and friends, and yet no one can read his books and his letters without feeling that he was somehow a man who had found his own felicity. He could even cheer his more fortunate but despairing friends! He could do what he loved best of all to do—live richly in his own mind. As one of his friends said of him, he had the "determination to win an honourable discharge in the bankrupt business of human life."

With that I began to reflect that so many men have owed their lasting contributions to the wealth of the race to some unhappy adventure of health or of fortune, some catastrophe of imprisonment or banishment, wherein, having mastered their own spirits, they were at length able to live a complete life. I think it was in prison that Cervantes wrote *Don Quixote;* and Paul addressed some of the best of his letters from Roman jails. Old Chinese poetry, released to us now by Arthur Waley and others, was often written while the authors were in banishment. It is a pity that the fashion of putting poets and prophets in jail should have waned: we might now be producing masterpieces!

A book I have included for many years upon my most intimate shelf is one that is all too little known. It is called *Some Fruits of Solitude* and was written by William Penn, the Quaker, during the time that he was banished from the court. A useful man, William Penn, a figure in American history, but he will live longest I think for the writings of those months or years of fruitful solitude when he had been forcibly banished from the world and had leisure to look into his own thoughts. In his introduction to this masterpiece of courage and common sense, he speaks of solitude as "a School few care to learn in, tho' None instructs us better." His various imprisonments and his banishment do not crush him: he "blesseth God for his Retirement, and kisses the Gentle Hand which led him into it: For though it prove Barren to the World, it can never do so to him."

He goes on to tell of some of the advantages of enforced solitude:

"He has now had some Time he could call his own; a Property he was never so much Master of before: In which he has taken a View of himself and the World; and observed wherein he hath hit and mist the mark."

And what does he find? He is so far from being overborne or cast down by his experiences that he is sometimes close to exultation that he is able to be quiet, remarking quaintly:

"But after we have made the just Reckonings which Retirement will help us to we shall begin to think the World in great measure Mad, and that we have been in a sort of Bedlam all this while."

A little later, when I was able to get this book again into my hands, I remember the good laugh I had over this passage. Is it possible to reach a higher point of satisfied comfort, especially in jail, than to think one's self quite sane and all the world else in a "great measure Mad"?

So it was that I considered, as I lay there

through the long days and nights—and not
without satisfaction—that so much of the great
and good work in the world has been done by
men in trouble, themselves full of suffering and
sorrow.

Two or three times I caught myself positively
enjoying these meditations, my illness for the
moment quite forgotten. I could sometimes con-
tinue for an hour or so, wholly absorbed, before
weariness and weakness overcame me. When
I awakened in the night it was no longer to the
bored misery of the earlier days, but to a new
interest, a fresh hope. There seemed something
now to live for: something even to be achieved,
for was not my felicity still to be made or
found? If I had to lie there in bed, there must be
a way to do it with a tranquil if not triumphant
mind.

After a time the Tyrant of that place decreed
that I might have Books—not too many, I was
warned, but Books. I think I had never been so
long before in my life without a book or books
within reach of my outstretched hand. I am one
of those who loves to carry a little book in his

pocket: and there is always a book or so on the stand at the head of my bed at night, or by the couch where I so easily sit down to read by day. It was a great moment for me, then, when I could look forward to having a favourite book in my hand.

"I am," I said to myself, "like the man condemned to live on a lonely isle, with only two or five or ten books to comfort him. What a difficult but beautiful time he would have in selecting them."

I began at once, and with a pleasure I cannot describe, to think what books I should send for. No books by sickly men: no books by little, whining men: no invented books. Such vast libraries there were, I did not want! What I longed for, there in my imprisonment, were robust, courageous books, books that would stay the soul of a man. Old, strong, brave books! Books that were the true "life blood of a master spirit," written out of the travail of living, full of the experience of one brave in spite of pain and certain failure. There are not too many of them in the world: a modest shelf or so, I think, would hold them all. There are harmless lesser books enough to beguile a man's hours, books to dally over, to relieve the tedium of a journey, but when one is face to face with the stark reality of life it is not such that one hungers for.

The book I thought of first, since it appealed to the need of the moment, has for years been one of my closest companions. I had now a longing for it that was as intense as any primitive appetite, and, oddly enough, not alone for its contents, but for the book itself—the look of it, the feel of it in my hand as it slid into my pocket. A good appetite is one of the rewards of hunger : and my deprivation had aroused such a sharpness of desire as I had never before felt for any book. This was my small, thin pocket edition, printed on India paper, of *The Thoughts of the Emperor M. Aurelius Antoninus.* I remember well when and where I got it; it was in the year 1902, at a bookshop in Charing Cross Road in London. A long time ago! I had never read it before that time, but extracts or aphorisms, cast out as the skilled

angler casts a fly, upon the wide and turbulent
waters of the daily press, or in the quieter pools
of books or magazines, I had sometimes
snapped at, since they seemed food agreeable
to my taste. One or two such passages lay warm
in my mind and had stayed me in times of per-
plexity.

"Live as on a mountain."

"If any man has done wrong, the harm is his
own. But perhaps he has not done wrong."

"Dost thou wish to be praised by a man who
curses himself thrice every hour?"

It was a charming small book bound in dark
red cloth with the name *Marcus Aurelius
Antoninus* in gilded Roman letters on the cover.
It cost me, as I remember, three shillings, as
good a value for the money as ever I had of a
purchase. It contained an essay on the life and
philosophy of the noble emperor by George
Long, who was also the translator of the text.

Other books for other needs or other moods,
but no book I know contains more powerfully
set forth the philosophy of endurance. It is a
great and beautiful thing to enjoy life—and I,

in my time, have had much enjoyment of life. It is still a greater thing to endure life—endure it not fiercely, not grievously, but with equanimity. This small book, written while the Emperor was far away from Rome, in a kind of kingly slavery to his responsibilities, fighting the wild Quadi, I have read when hard pressed with labour, when I was hurt or sad or ill or lonely. It served well, a pocket companion, in the miserable months I spent in Europe during the Great War. Of all the noble books of the world none I know seems so clearly written by the author not to instruct, still less to enthrall others, but for himself and to himself. He addresses himself, admonishes himself, reassures himself: it is his way of fortifying his own soul. Much reading of both Marcus Aurelius and Epictetus, whose philosophy is practically identical, inclines me always to the Emperor rather than to the slave: for Epictetus was discoursing for the improvement of his followers, but Marcus Aurelius for the discipline of his own spirit. It is not a book to bow down before and worship—what book is?—

but a book to use when there is the deep need of it; and it is the spirit of the man, not the letter of his philosophy, which heals.

It was this small book, then, that I put at the top of my list. To that I added William Penn's book, which I have already mentioned, and an anthology containing much of the noblest thought in the world—*The Spirit of Man,* edited by Robert Bridges, recently poet laureate of England. All these were books that I could read a little at a time, as I had strength. I also asked for Shakespeare's *Tempest,* and for a quaint book of travel, because I had long loved the author in other books, *The Bible in Spain,* by George Borrow. There were still others in the list I may mention later: and from another source I had several books by Dr. William Osler which had in them not only the true quality I required, but subjects treated which, being now myself in a hospital, I found enormously interesting. One of them was called *An Alabama Student.* A Bible I wanted also, for I had the appetite to read the Book of Job straight through.

"Have you by any chance," I asked my nurse, "among the many valuable medicines in your cabinet—have you a Bible?"

"A Bible!"

"Yes," said I, "a Bible."

So she brought me next morning her own Bible, and in the days following—slowly, slowly—I read the Book of Job, and some of the Psalms, and certain chapters of Isaiah, and Ecclesiastes, and the first book of the Corinthians.

What a book it is! Full of wisdom and beauty, ripe with human nature—if only one does not use it for a fetish or look into it for magic.

From this time onward, and with these weapons, I began to have oases in the desert of my illness.

V   THE STARLINGS

V

THE STARLINGS

I could not think so plain a bird
Could sing so fine a song.

ONE morning early, after I had been in that place for some time, I heard through the open window the sweet, familiar whistle of a quail. Bob-*white:* bob-*white.* At first I could not believe my ears. There in that city! What place or part had a shy meadow bird like the quail in such a maze of city streets and rumbling car lines and close-built houses? It could not be possible. I listened intently and with a curious warmth around the heart. There it was again, thrillingly wild and sweet: bob-*white,* bob-*white.* It brought back to me with vivid pain the memory of the long sloping meadows I have known so well, and my own lanes and wooded hills where in spring one may start the nesting quail running as though wounded in the grass, or in autumn flush a new covey.

When I had heard the starlings at my window a week or so earlier I had closed my ears and eyes. I did not like starlings: I did not like to have reminders of the free world I could not enjoy. But the song of the quail, rich with old memories and warm associations, was quite another matter.

A little later on the same morning—before the day nurse came in and everything was quiet —I was further amazed to hear another and dearly familiar bird note: Pee-a-wee, pee-a-wee! —the plaintive call of the modest little fly-catcher I had so often watched flitting about in the brushy edges of old fields. But what could the pee-wee be doing here? And why her song, so full of lazy melancholy, at this time of the year? And how was it possible that I, through my open window, among the treetops, could catch it all so clearly?

It was one of those delightful country queries that I had, in times past, so often found alluring. For a time, that morning, I not only forgot my discomforts, but I forgot also the books with which I had begun to occupy my mind.

"This morning," I said to my nurse, "I heard a quail whistling through the open window. Are there quail among these houses?"

I asked the same question of the knowing doctor, and the efficient head nurse, and the broadly smiling Negro janitor: but not one of them had ever seen or heard of any quail in that neighbourhood. There was something about their responses, something indulgent and yet faintly skeptical, that a sick man learns to know.

"Nevertheless," said I, "I heard a quail whistling."

That day I did not read much out of *Lavengro,* nor consider, as I had intended, the saying of Marcus Aurelius which seemed to speak so aptly to my present condition. I was not indeed able to read much, so I read deeply, keeping each choice morsel long in my mind that I might extract its last savour. In times past I

had been accustomed to take a book as it were
by storm, tearing the heart out of it, and scat-
tering the tattered remains wherever they might
chance to fall. Many books, most books, deserve
no better attention: but it is no way to treat
any book that is really worth the reading. For
when a truly great spirit, with labour, and with
pain, and with joy, has put his life blood into
his work, it is only with labour and with pain
and with joy that the reader may recover it
again. Great things are never to be had without
paying for them.

So it is that one may read for three minutes
in, say, Marcus Aurelius, and have something
to stay him for an hour or a day. The passage
to which I have referred was this:

"Wretch, are you not content with what you
see daily? Have you anything better or greater
to see than the sun, the moon, the stars, the
whole earth, the sea?"

It was true; it was true. I had been lying
here these weeks, wretch that I was, consumed
by my own ills, allowing my own miserable past
and my own anxious future to blot out the sun,

the moon, the stars, the whole earth, the sea. I was not content with what I could see daily. The present moment, this burning instant of time, was all that I or any man could ever really possess or command—and I was allowing it to be ruined by anxieties that were of my own making. It had come to me, powerfully, that if I could be content at *this* moment, I could be content.

It was in the atmosphere of these reflections that I heard, in the early morning, the bird notes I have described, as they came to me through the open window. They came to me sweetly, thrillingly. "Have you anything," I asked myself, "better or greater to see or to hear than this? Why not, man, enjoy it? Can you not be content with what you see daily?"

All that forenoon it seemed to me that something pleasant had, at length, come to me. A touch of my old enthusiasm! Something rare and fine. So little there is to occupy the attention of a man who is ill in bed.

I had a restless night—"You are too intense," said the nurse; "you are under some strain"—but the following morning—she did not know!—as soon as it was fairly light I propped up my pillows so that I could the better look out of the open window into the treetops. I was eager with an eagerness I cannot describe to hear again the whistling of the quail and the plaintive cry of the wood peewee. It seemed somehow to me then a way out of my distress.

I waited impatiently for some time, and then, to my distaste, I saw that the English starlings had come to sit on the boughs of the beech tree which reached so near my window. I was thoroughly disappointed—when I had expected so much. As I have said, I did not like starlings. I considered them alien invaders. They had come only recently to my own neighbourhood, and I had found them boisterous and unmannerly. They had driven out a friendly pair of bluebirds that nested in a hollow apple tree not far from my doorway; they had stolen my cherries, pecked into my grapes, and one cold winter morning, I remember, I found a large flock of them in my hen house, perched in every conceivable spot, even on the roosts among the fowls. When

I opened the door they rose with a tremendous whirr and dove straight through the meshes of the wire netting that screened the front of the building, meshes that, it would have seemed, no bird could creep through, much less fly through. It was a feat to see! Nor did I like the raucous cry of warning or alarm with which they filled the very air. How much more modest and charming, I thought, are our own bluebirds and orioles and catbirds and song sparrows, to say nothing of that golden songster the wood thrush.

And yet here they were this morning on the bough by the window. "Wretch," I said to myself, "are you not content with what you see daily? Are there no beauties or interests in this world that you have not already discovered?"

With that I began to observe the starlings more closely. The sun was just coming up, filtering through the lacy fretwork of beech twigs, and I caught the glint of colour on their wings and back. I had always thought of them as a kind of rusty black—so they had appeared in the spring and summer flocks I had seen oftenest—but they were not so at all upon close observation. Quite otherwise, indeed, for they were clad in shimmering garments of iridescent blue, steel green, purple, with here and there, especially when they moved, the glint of a buff-tipped wing feather. The breasts were mottled with splashes of white or buff. In all these discoveries I was vastly surprised and interested.

I began to watch them still more closely. What active, sprightly fellows they were, anyway! There was something jaunty, almost humorous, in the way they sidled about, cocked their heads, preened their feathers. I had thought them unmannerly and raucous-voiced, but there was something positively charming in the little intimate, almost affectionate airs they put on as they sat together exchanging the gossip of a fine autumn morning. And so far from the harsh cries I knew them by I now heard, from my highly privileged place, their deliciously intimate conversation. They too, like our own native catbirds and thrushes, had their low whisper songs, though with them it was scarcely song at all, but low, musical ejaculations and gurgling notes, and from time to time, as though some of the gossip had passed utterly beyond the pale of credibility or propriety, some bird would break in with a kind of ironical whistle, high, clear, and sweet, and as it seemed to me that morning, full of laughter. They reminded me exactly of a group of lively old ladies, all by themselves, at a tea party.

I have been interested all my life in birds— as an amateur enjoyer rather than a careful student—and it seemed to me that morning that no birds I had known before gave such an impression of distinct and vigorous *personality* as these. They had such a gift of being entirely alive and joyous in a world that I had begun to think unhealthy and abnormal. They seemed actually to have a kind of humour!

These impressions came to me with something of a shock considering the contempt in which I had previously held them: but it was as nothing compared with the shock that I had a little later.

While I was thus observing the starlings as closely as I could I heard again the note of our meadow quail: bob-*white,* bob-*white.* It was perfectly clear and distinct. I was greatly excited.

"There," said I, "I knew perfectly well I heard it."

And a little later, to my surprise, came the song of my old friend the wood pee-wee. Pee-a-wee, pee-a-wee!

They seemed close at hand, as though the birds were under or near my window. Just at that moment one of the starlings ruffled the feathers of its throat in song, and though at first I could scarcely credit my senses, it seemed evident that my bob-white was in reality a starling! It was a thrilling moment. Was it possible? Was my pee-wee also a starling? I listened and watched again with great intentness and soon assured myself that the starlings, in addition to many other gifts, were also mocking-birds.

I don't wonder that my nurse shook her head over me that morning—though I lay there as quietly and innocently as though I did not feel like Byrd and Peary and Edison all rolled into one.

"Quiet," she cautioned, "quiet."

"No one," said I, "could have been quieter than I, and it has brought me great things."

"Great things?" she asked.

"Very great things," said I, but I did not then tell her what they were.

The next morning I was again awake at dawn, but doomed to sharp disappointment, for the starlings, which I began now to think of as old friends, did not appear. A drizzling rain fell all day long. On the second morning, however, I was delighted to find the plump little old ladies gathering for their tea party. It may seem ridiculous, but my heart beat more quickly, and I had a delightful sense of anticipation, for I had begun to love them. What busybodies they were! It was not the mating season, nor yet the gala time of year when the happy business of feeding the young birds is afoot: but the starlings, apparently without a care or responsibility in the world, were nevertheless enjoying themselves prodigiously, exchanging the most

delicious bits of gossip, mimicking their neighbours and whistling ironically to one another
when the conversation became too incredible—
or scandalous—for belief. Lines from a poem
on the starling I have since discovered express
exactly my wonder:

> All this April rollicking
> In the last month of the year
> Has no logic I can see.

How pleasant and yet how rare it is, whether
among birds or men, to find such a mood of
easy enjoyment where there is neither love-
making nor business in hand! Enjoyment of the
delightful little daily things of life: a fine morning, good companions, the sound of one's own
songs!

VI ADVENTURES ABROAD IN BED

VI

ADVENTURES ABROAD IN BED

It is by studying little things that we attain the great art
of having as little misery and as much happiness as possible.
Samuel Johnson, BOSWELL, Vol. I, p. 288.

MY INTEREST in the starlings grew
rapidly, and because I felt that I had so
wronged them in my early judgment I wanted
to know much more about them—as we do
about friends we are coming to love. Were they
really mockers? And what other birds did they
mimic? Were they the destroyers and pests I
had always thought them? And where did they
come from and how?

"Will you do me an especial favour?" I
asked my excellent and obliging nurse.

"I will indeed," said she.

So I asked her to write to the ornithologist
at Washington and see if there was not some

bulletin or pamphlet on the starling which we could obtain. It was long in coming—a sick man grows impatient—but it arrived at last, and it had a portrait of my friend on the cover. It was an excellent and expansive study of the bird, some thirty pages, which my nurse read aloud to me, a little at a time. It seems that the bird has been a native of America only since 1890, when it settled, an encouraged immigrant, in Central Park, New York. Like many another alien, it had a struggle for years to live, but presently it began to spread into other Eastern states, and it is now increasing even beyond the Alleghany Mountains. In time it will no doubt become one of our commonest American birds. I was pleased to find that, despite certain harmful and unmannerly habits—don't we all have them?—it is economically a most useful citizen of the country, destroying innumerable insects that infest our farms and gardens.

In one way this excellent biography of my friend the starling did not satisfy me. It resembled some other lives of the poets I have sadly read, like one of Shelley from which I emerged, dripping with facts, but unable to understand how any such person could possibly have written the ode "To a Skylark." I was not unmindful of the patience of the investigators in counting the number of weevils, grubs, and millipeds that my hero had for breakfast, but it no more explained to me some of the things I wanted to know than an accurate count of the yards of spaghetti Caruso ate for supper would have accounted for his singing, not long afterwards, of an aria from *Aïda*.

But it was a fine and interesting book, and so aroused our enthusiasm that it was not long before my gifted nurse, sitting at the window, could mimic the ironical whistle of the starlings so accurately that she was accepted as an honorary member of their tea parties: at least, her notes were promptly answered. Soon our book was in circulation through other rooms in the hospital, and more than one patient began to listen to the morning meetings of the starlings.

A most interesting and surprising characteristic of the starlings I have observed more closely since I left the hospital—and that is the evolutions of large flocks of the birds in the air. The precision and discipline are truly extraordinary—the way in which they will suddenly change direction, open ranks, close ranks, wheel, rise, fall, all in perfect unison, and so far as I have been able to observe, without any one leader and without any note or cry of command. No flocking birds I know have greater gifts in this respect: and nothing except the extraordinary social discipline of bees and ants is more inexplicable. There is a secret of mass movement, a guidance of mass opinion, that is as yet unknown to man. I wonder if some social philosopher, one day, will not wish to study faithfully the gregarious habits—the "mob psychology!"—of such birds as the starling and of the bees and ants.

My morning experiences were not only a source of comfort and delight to me in that sorrowy place, but they opened the way to new adventures. Adventures abroad in bed! The nurse did not see me, nor the doctors know of it, nor was it written down in the sober sheets

of my daily record, but I was going out again!
Though covered to the chin with a white
counterpane, apparently quite helpless, I was
in reality often abroad among my own hills,
or in my garden, or walking the pleasant elm-
shaded streets of the little town I love best of
all. I don't mean by this any mere darting
memories, full of sadness or regret, I mean that
I was *there*. I was there to complete absorption,
so that I was not conscious for the time being
of the gabled room where I lay, nor of the hospital, nor of my own illness.

It was all simple enough. I would, in my
imagination, step out of my doorway, and there
—oh, vividly!—was the garden, and the
orchard, and the meadow, and far beyond, the
everlasting hills. The steps and the path being
open before me, what could I do but walk down
it? And walking down it, what could I do but
look at, or smell, or touch, the various shrubs,
flowers, trees, I love?—or the corn, or the black-
berry bushes, or the nut trees, dear with the
familiarity of many years of intimate association.

Such moments—most of all in May—watching the young bees playing in front of the hives, and the catbirds in the apple trees, singing like angels in heaven—and stealing the bees!—and the tulips in bloom, and the new corn pushing up through the brown earth, and the newly sowed grassland coming green with clover and timothy and red-top—and all still and sweet. Such moments in a sunny forenoon.

Sometimes as I lay there a past experience or adventure would return to me with such intensity of remembrance that it seemed to me I was living it again. One in particular, since it was so charged with emotion, I tried to put down in the notebook I had begun to keep in the little desk at the head of my bed.

A certain old barn I love well. A great, gray old barn, reaching out its sheds like wings on either side to hover the cattle when they come in at evening with swinging udders, smelling of new milk. I love the cavernous open doorway where the barn swallows fly chittering in and out. I love the dusty smell of hay as I step inside. . . .

I can hear the horses stirring in their stanchions below—and the cows coming in to their stalls. . . .

Up there toward the west a finger of sunlight reaches through a crack and lies bright upon the hills of hay. These are hewn beams: you can see each stroke of the broad-axe, or adz. . . .

A flood of sunshine comes through the farther doorway. From within, looking out, I can see the pleasant rolling country, fine fields, and verdure-clad hills, with the sun upon them. The wind runs sweet in the grass, the crows are flying. There is no frame made by man that can equal the doorway of this barn, and no picture anywhere so well worth the framing. . . .

Here in the barn I stand looking, remembering. There is the well worn farm wagon with the hayrack still upon it; there the buggy covered with cloth to keep the dust away. . . .

Upon the wooden door of the storeroom

generations of Dwights have marked the score
of corn in baskets or rye in bags, four straight
tallies and a cross tally to make five. Here they
have added up the totals and sometimes cast
them into the sure measure of dollars and
cents. . . .

On the left, here, is the ancient harness room
where, upon great wooden pegs worn brown
and smooth with years of usage, hang the col-
lared harnesses, the horse blankets, a girl's
saddle. . . .

(It was Nanette's—I remember well Nanette,
with the wind in her hair, and the high look in
her eyes as she rode.)

And here is all that remains of a pony cart.
(It was Lauriston's.) It was gay once with
paint, and there was a fancy name on the back,
but now the padded seat is torn, and one of the
thills is gone. (Lauriston lies in a hillside grave
in France.)

I could not go on. . . .

All these things, and many others, came back

to me as I lay there in bed, charged with emotion, tinged with strange sadness—moments in which nothing of any importance had happened, and yet so intensely lived that they returned with a warmth and clarity I can scarcely express.

So it was, now that I had found the way, that I began adventuring abroad in bed.

VII THE AUTOBIOGRAPHY OF MY HEART

VII

THE AUTOBIOGRAPHY OF MY HEART

Call to recollection both how many things thou hast passed
through, and how many things thou hast been able to endure
. . . and how many beautiful things thou hast seen. . . .

I COME now to one of my choicest adventures
while I lay there ill in that high-gabled room.
For adventure is not outside a man; it is within.
It is a strange thing, once the mind goes free,
what may happen to any man. Space and time
are both forgot. Lying close in bed a man can
in an instant be walking in his own distant
garden, or, stripping away the crowded years,
find himself the boy he knew so long ago.

What one sees in a hospital—men lying there
inert, waiting to live again or to die—is as nothing compared with what goes on there. What
adventures all unrecorded, what dramas un-

acted or tragedies unwept, what secret laughter, what bitter curses, what remorse, what fear, what hope, what hot tears under smarting eyelids—and all covered and concealed from the probings of even the skilfulest of physicians, withheld from the most sympathetic of nurses. To some men the experience of being thus driven in upon themselves is one of bitterness, even of terror; to others it comes as a fruitful opportunity, for "nowhere either with more quiet or more freedom from trouble does a man retire than into his own soul." And some to whom the experience is at first bitter to the point of being unbearable, are able, presently, to direct their minds so that they have "such thoughts that by looking into them" they are "immediately in perfect tranquillity" for as this philosopher further remarks, "tranquillity is nothing else than the good ordering of the mind."

And the renewal comes not alone from reflection upon "principles brief and fundamental," but upon free excursions of the mind in all directions, particularly in that strange and vivid

reliving, possible to any man, of the most interesting or happiest incidents of his own life,
those moments, let us say, that he himself, in
his inmost thoughts, considers best.

In my own case I found it delightful to go
back to my youth. I came, indeed, upon the
train of the adventure I am about to narrate,
while I was endeavouring, as I have already
related, to recapture the poetry I had known in
my boyhood. It had led me naturally to the
thought of the tall, dark old bookcase standing
atop a "secretary" that stood in my father's
house. It had a carved head of Shakespeare
looking down from the pediment above the
glass doors. My father was a sturdy old Presby-
terian, and there were shelves devoted to
Kitto's Commentaries on the Bible, Cruden's
Concordance, and a volume of Fox's Martyrs,
that had belonged, I think, to his father—in the
horrors of which I thoroughly delighted—and
I know not how many volumes of other religious
books. But there was also a shelf of Scott's
novels, in green cloth binding with a globe on
the cover, and Dickens and Shakespeare, and

stray volumes of Bulwer Lytton and George
Eliot and other Victorian writers. There was a
close-print Plutarch bound in leather, which I
now have, a prized book, on my own shelves,
and *Pilgrim's Progress,* and *Don Quixote,* and
Twenty Thousand Leagues Under the Sea, and
Plato's *Republic* and a set of Ancient Classics
in English translations, and Byron and Felicia
Hemans and Martin Tupper. How vividly I remember my father reading in bed: his leonine
head propped up on the pillows, a kerosene lamp,
shaded from his eyes, placed upon his breast,
and the book held strongly in one hand—the
other steadying the lamp—while he read far
along into the night.

How eagerly, lying there in that hospital
room, I revisited the old black bookcase. I could
go there with my eyes shut, open the glass doors,
and put my hand on any book in it that I cared
for—not Cruden's Concordance, nor Kitto's
Commentaries! I opened them now and from
the third shelf, in the corner, for it was a shabby
book, I took out the volume I was seeking. One
of the corners of the binding was bent over and

worn down until the brown board within was plainly visible. It looked as though it had been gnawed. In this old book I found, beginning exactly where I knew it would on the page, a poem by an author now known not at all as a poet but as the biographer of Sir Walter Scott. I mean John Gibson Lockhart. In those days I knew nothing and cared less for the names or accomplishments of authors. Smith was as full of significance for me as Shakespeare. I was intent upon the thing itself. I knew what I wanted, that was literature, all the world of writing else was trash. I have wondered sometimes if I was not a better judge then than I am now.

The poem I speak of was from the Spanish Ballads, and at the first lines of it all my years dropped suddenly away, and I was fourteen years old, thrilling again with an experience I shall never forget.

> My ornaments are arms,
>   My pastime is in war;
> My bed is cold upon the wold,
>   My lamp yon star.

It was in the evening, I remembered, that I first came upon it, and it went straight to my head, like some divine intoxicant. After finishing the entire poem in one delicious draught I shut the book with a snap, seized my cap, and dashed out of the house. A young moon hung in the clear autumn sky; the silence of evening lay deep upon the world; cool airs had followed the heat of the day. So I walked, or ran, chanting to myself:

> "My ornaments are arms,
>   My pastime is in war;
> My bed is cold upon the wold,
>   My lamp yon star."

I don't think I knew what "wold" meant, but it is one of the charms of poetry—at fourteen —that you do not understand it all. Worlds thus open to a word! And as I ran, the last verse also I chanted:

> "I ride from land to land,
>   I sail from sea to sea;
> Some day more kind I fate may find,
>   Some night kiss thee!"

And is not that the beautiful end of adventure
—at fourteen!

Some night kiss thee!

I had not thought of this incident before in
years and it came over me now with a delight
that was also full of sadness:

> Ah those days beyond renewing
> Days the prime of love and lovely——

It was this incident, and especially the
thought of the charm I had found so long ago
in the word "wold," as it appeared in the verse
I have mentioned, that set me thinking one night
of the strange love affairs one may have with
beautiful or desirable words. So many incidents
crowded at once upon me that I began to consider the writing of Confessions, like Rousseau,
or better yet, a kind of Sentimental Journey
among words, in which, with a total disregard
for all the proprieties, and flinging reticence
quite to the winds, I should set down my love
affairs—how it was that in my travels through

the world I met this charmer or that, what it was that caught my wandering fancy and how it was held.

"It must," I said to myself with keen joy in the idea, "be a new kind of autobiography of the heart."

VIII MANY THINGS I PASSED
THROUGH

VIII

MANY THINGS I PASSED THROUGH

Take my hand quick and tell me,
What have you in your heart?

I BEGAN to think, as I lay there in bed, and with a delight impossible to convey, how I had thrown my heart away, in years past, upon one darling word after another. Nearly always it had been a case of love at first sight, and it came with such inexpressible charm that I could scarcely let the loved one a moment from my presence. How I contrived beautiful sentences wherein to mount it like a jewel, or spacious paragraphs to house it in. Age, I had learned in these chance meetings, quite contrary to the more prosaic love affairs of ordinary life, counted for nothing whatever. I had fallen desperately to the charm of a word that was a good five hundred years old, one that Chaucer knew when he rode to Canterbury with his quaint pilgrims; and a day or so later, perhaps in the rebound, I had been hopelessly enslaved by a kind of modern flapper word, as young as the twentieth century, met on the streets of New York—an impudent hussy who winked at me scandalously in broad daylight as I passed. And sometimes, and these are half-guilty meetings, had I stolen at the very wedding, like some young Lochinvar, the bride of another writer, knowing her for mine, as she knew me, upon sight.

Upon this I began to think of one of my more recent infatuations and the amusing outcome of it. I had been reading some verses which had in them, for me, a bewitching music when the fatal meeting took place. The word literally leaped at me out of the printed page, bringing with it a strange air of dark-winged mystery—full of low music. This was the verse I read:

Ah! Strange were the dim, wide meadows,
And strange was the cloud-strewn sky,
And strange in the meadows the corncrakes
And they making cry!

Of course, the word was "corncrakes," which never in my life had I heard before. It was not that the word itself was charming or even comely—but it carried such a wild, free, mysterious air! Crying strangely, it was, in dim, wide meadows, with the sky above cloud-strewn! Why had I never before met this beguiling word? I loved it for its mystery, and at first went about with it often upon my tongue, or in my thoughts, for the thrill it gave me. Nor did I care at first for closer knowledge. Too intimate acquaintance, I have found, often dissipates the mystery of words not less than that of human beings. Some words are best left free in the place where they live—say in a stanza of poetry—for the complete impression, or feeling, they give us. Let them go on living, strange in the dim, wide meadows . . . and they making cry!

But human nature is perverse, and if left with the key will be forever peeping in at Bluebeard's secret door. And so it was that finally, my curiosity getting the better of the thrill, I opened my unimpeachable dictionary—that enemy of mystery, that destroyer of charm, that matter-of-fact abolisher of all half lights and strange, dim meadows. (I say abolish all dictionaries: and will myself head an organized movement to do it!)

Well, I laughed—a little ruefully—when I found that my corncrake was only "a common European bird, the land rail"—but that's the way of life. Our corncrakes are forever turning common birds. And so it was that my sudden infatuation vanished: and though, as I thought of it, I loved still the music of the verse, I could not get the same thrill of it now that I saw only common birds in those strange, dim meadows.

But if some of the love affairs I remembered had been swift, passionate, and too brief, like this one—soon in love, soon out of it!—I recalled others that had lasted all my life, and will, I think truly, when I am still older and grayer, touch my lips and stir my heart.

The story of one of them was truly a story of early love: a word I grew up with, knew and worshipped in school, walked with through many a starry night of my dreamy youth, and

have with me yet, a dear companion. A word
may sometimes be knit into the very soul of a
man, and mean to him a whole life of wonder
and adventure. I have heard people tell of
"acquiring a language." It cannot be done: a
language must be lived.

I came of pioneer stock. Each generation of
my family stepped one long step westward, following the receding frontier. The appetite for
going on, the far look to the setting sun, is
deep in my race. You can see it in the eyes of
my race. When I was a boy there was always
talk in my home of the great things that lay
just beyond—beyond the horizon, beyond this
troubled life! (The promises of their reli-
gion bound the pioneers to its tenets.) Here
life was hard; men toiled wearily in the new
land; they fought poverty and isolation with
grim-jawed courage—and fed their starving
souls upon deferred joy. But one could always
go on to the West, where the land would be
richer than it was here, where men would be
freer and bolder, where wealth could be had for
the taking. All this lay beyond the horizon, and

the name given to this joyous, far Utopia, this land of promise, was "the Plains." The Plains beyond: one could go on to the Plains.

When I was a boy we had many a vivid and surprising demonstration of the wonders of the Plains. Our men went there to hunt the wild buffalo, and sometimes met still wilder Indians. They brought back robes and mounted heads and horns as trophies, and still more marvellous tales of adventure they brought back. On the Plains men had not to hew their way through heavy forests or toil upon the bitter hills: one had only to stake out the open land and turn wide the waiting soil!

Once a wonderful covered wagon, which to a boy's fancy was a caravan of pure joy, crept across the hills from the East, and swaying and tacking like a ship at sea, held its course into the West and went down with the sun. I remember the dusty, bronzed, and silent skipper of this desert ship; and the women in their sunbonnets and calico dresses. I suspect the hardened eye of manhood would see them bedraggled and sad-looking, but they had for me at that time a kind of prophetic beauty. They were headed into the sunset: they were going on to the Plains.

It is easy to see what beauty and mystery came to be bound up, for an imaginative boy, in that beautiful word. It was a symbol of adventure, of free open spaces, clear air, and blue heavens, boundlessly high; it was the sign of the noble and spacious life. Here at home one was bound down to the trivial and ugly—one had to carry water daily in a tin pail from a distant spring at the foot of the hill; one had to feed the pigs and bed down the horses—but there, where the wind blew in the grass, and there were no hills anywhere to hem one in, but only space and thought, one could run and sing! And somehow, and I speak of this as diffidently as men speak of the deeper things in their lives—but it is true—I thought God must be there more than here. For where everything is free and beautiful and noble—is not God there? It seemed the only place I knew where there was enough room for God.

I wondered as I lay there in my bed why some of our American poets had not seized more

often upon this beautiful word which represents, with its associations, so much of the true
genius and inspiration of our own people. I
remembered one such stanza—a single stanza,
the author of which I never knew, nor could
find out—which had lain for years like a jewel
in my mind:

> I am the Plain, virgin since Time began,
> Yet do I dream of Motherhood, when Man
> One day at last shall look upon my charms,
> And give me Towns like children to my arms.

All these things, then, were tied up in that
single word "Plains"—the Plain—which I had
never heard without the kind of thrill which
comes at the stirring of an old love—an old, old
love. And, indeed, it had acquired values that it
never had before: because love, if it is true love,
lifts, as the years pass, from the literal and
physical which early charm us, to other, finer,
sweeter, deeper beauty. My Plains had now lost
their buffalo, the last Indian had shot his arrow
and vanished beyond the rolling horizon, the
blowing grass had been turned under with

chilled-iron ploughs—but still I had my Plains. I had my Plains: but they were Plains now of the spirit, that the spirit would be yearning for, where all was spacious and free, and men were noble, and the wind of great thought blew through the sunny grass, and God dwelt.

So it was that I spent not a little time, during those days and nights of my illness, calling to recollection many things I had passed through. Often I found myself so completely absorbed as to be quite unconscious of my condition. Especially was this true after I began to be able to write down a few notes regarding my experiences. At times I wearied of these excursions and found myself slipping back into the depressed consciousness of my weakness and discomfort, but as the weeks passed I found it easier and easier to bridge the gaps. I found myself better prepared to meet the ordeal that was to come.

IX THE GREAT HOSPITAL

IX

THE GREAT HOSPITAL

Where a man can live, there he can also live well.

IT SEEMED a strange, vast, grim place, my hospital, when at length I came to meet the supreme test for which I had been so long preparing. It was at first incredibly forbidding to me—the very cleanness of it, the bright efficiency, the ceremonial smile it wore. One instinctively shrinks from pain, yet pain, perhaps even more the fear of it, is here the badge of the initiate, the ritual of proficiency. I had the sense of being irresistibly drawn into a process that was inimical and yet inevitable. I had no longer any volition so far as my body was concerned: it was moved about like so much inert material by forces presumably intelligent but wholly outside myself. I was no longer asked whether I wanted this or would do that: I was not talked to, I was talked about.

"At five you may give him the drops; after that he is to have nothing."

The narrow white bed I lay upon was a symbol of the extremity I had reached, for my head was lifted or my legs adjusted not by any will of my own but by an iron crank at the foot of it, turned by the white-clad nurse. When the time came, I would be lifted from my bed, still more inert, laid upon a table—and the surgeon would be there.

My reaction to these indignities was somewhat surprising to me. Why was I not angry or terrified or crushed? I had been far more nearly overborne when I had lain down, weeks before, in the room with the gabled window. No doubt I had gained something of self-possession in those weeks, some added power of living with equanimity in my own mind, and yet, much as I should like to take the credit, I do not think my attitude was due to self-discipline. One rises to an emergency; he does what he must; a soldier will rush into battle with colours flying who has suffered all the pangs of fear in waiting for the battle to begin.

It was a strange thing to me indeed—I am trying to set forth my exact thoughts—that I found myself, the inner core of me, taking very much the position that the doctors themselves took. This body of mine, this poor defective body that I carried about with me, was something separate, something inert though living, that could be observed dispassionately, treated objectively. *Me*—I was something apart, a detached identity, curled up in my own place—where *is* that place?—peering out at the doctors, the nurses, the little room, and my own body lying there on the queer, cranked bed. *I* was perfectly well: it was my body that was suffering. I was living and thinking with a power and vividness they could know nothing about.

Such a welter of swift thoughts! At the same moment that I was reassuring myself of my own independence and sufficiency, I was also pitying myself, even calculating quite coldly upon the chances of the operation. If I was afraid, I was

also thinking ironically of the absurdity of the
entire process. These serious doctors, interested
in my "case," believing they could cure my body
without knowing me! These smiling nurses to
whom my situation, so vastly important to my
life, was all in the routine of the day! At times
I was miles away from the hospital, and all of
its sights and sounds and odours and discomforts: I was in my own garden, walking there,
and there were tall hollyhocks in bloom, and
flaming zinnias, and delphiniums still in flower
—and, oh, the blue of the distant hills! Or I was
talking familiarly with my friends and refer-
ring to the hospital as though it were something
quite distant and wholly immaterial. But always
I came back to the little room, and the queer
bed, and the nurses smiling there; always I
came back.

Above everything else in those days I was full
of a kind of still confidence that I can only call
faith—an immense faith. Without it, how could
any man live through such an experience, how
trust the most precious of his possessions out of
his own control? To surrender voluntarily one's

consciousness, to go down and down and down into the abysmal nothingness of anæsthesia, not knowing *certainly* whether it would be for hours or forever—what is that but an act of faith? Or, if a man goes down involuntarily, by terror and force, how is he better than a horse or a dog? I thought much in the long days of my illness how impossible it was for any human being to live without faith—faith somewhere, in something, in somebody. All that makes a man a man and not an animal is suffused with faith. Without it the individual is insane and society a chaos. With it, and in proportion to the vitality of it, there can be nobility, and peace, and serenity.

The day of supreme trial came at length. The doctor was unusually benign; the nurse, unusually cheerful. I knew! I was to have the ether early in the morning. . . .

I had a swift sense of a world that was incalculably dear to me somehow slipping out of my grasp. I was conscious of a swift procession of familiar figures, Harriet there, my old friend Dr. M——, and my father, strangely the *essence* of my father, saying as he once said, long ago, when I was in danger—I could hear the very tones of his voice—"Steady now, boy, steady." Moments of joy turned to exquisite pain! Somehow the mind, knowing how short the time is, and keyed to an intolerable clarity of emotion, selects only essentials. At such moments every man is an artist. I tried afterwards to jot down all the things that raced through my mind in that instant between consciousness and unconsciousness, but could not: a teeming world of them, a universe lived in a moment of time.

A day or so after I came out of the ether, having thought much of that strange experience, I said to my nurse:

"Did I speak to you—did I say anything—on my way to the operating room?"

"Oh, yes," said she indulgently.

I paused: but finally asked the question.

"What did I say?"

She was smiling, I thought ironically—a little superior!

"You said: 'You will not leave me: you will stay close by?'"

It was what I had felt; but I could not remember whether I had really said it. I was strongly moved: thinking how instinctively, when we feel ourselves drifting out, we reach for some human contact.

I had gone down into the oblivion at nine in the morning and came struggling out sometime after five in the afternoon. Someone was apparently lifting or twisting my head aside by main force, and I was unspeakably miserable, faint, weary. The place was too warm. It seemed as if someone were holding me down. It made me indignant, and I began to kick. A voice that seemed infinitely distant was saying:

"He is coming out."

At that a wave of intense irritation swept through me. I was being disgracefully treated! It was a terrific effort, but I said as angrily as I could manage:

"Why don't they go on with it? Why all this delay?"

"It's all over. You came through beautifully."

"All over!" I said incredulously.

"Yes, you're through. Everything is all right."

It was unbelievable. All through! And I had felt, or heard, or seen nothing. I was at the moment unspeakably wretched, nauseated, but there was balm in those words. In the miserable half-opiated hours that followed, when there seemed nothing that I could do, no position that I could take, that was not exquisitely painful or uncomfortable, I kept saying to myself: "All over. I'm through." I clung fatuously to the words, "You came through beautifully." In spite of everything there was hope! I did not know at the time that I had been on the operating table, under the hands of that masterly surgeon, for two hours and a half, and that one does not recover too speedily from such an experience. Nevertheless, the worst had come and gone.

I had also a scarcely definable sensation that gave me the greatest comfort. I had found myself again! A kind of warm welcome swept over me at recognizing the familiar personality I had felt slipping away from me, that I had trusted so fearfully out of my own control. It had come back! What if it had not come back?

A little later I had another and wholly unexpected source of comfort. One day when the assistant surgeon was bending over me, attending to the dressings, I noted a small white scar across his face. I asked him about it.

"Well," said he, "I have been through it, too."

"You have been operated on?" I exclaimed in the greatest astonishment.

"Indeed I have," said he.

It had actually never occurred to me before that a surgeon, pursuing his bloody career, might himself have to undergo the same sort of ordeal. There had been an element of the superhuman about the confident master of his art that was now dissipated. The tables had been turned on him: he was, after all, a man of flesh and blood. I had quite a new feeling toward the profession!

"Are you entirely well again?" I asked.

"Perfectly," he responded.

"Are you as strong as ever?" I asked.

"Stronger! I'm better than I ever was before in my life."

It was like a draught of wine to me! It may seem absurd, but the surgeon leaning over me, hurting me cruelly, appeared at that moment a kind of angel—I have laughed since when I thought of his beaming young face—but he had given me new hope. *He* had been through it: *he* was better than ever!

Hope, I thought, is like love: it is there all the time, oceans of it, but someone must touch it off, awaken it.

I may have "come through beautifully"; I did not know how slowly nature moves in mending man's ills.

X   A SHIP OF SOULS

X

A SHIP OF SOULS

Nay, in thy own mean perplexities, do thou thyself
but *hold thy tongue for one day.* . . .
Sartor Resartus, Chapter III.

MY OPERATION produced a subtle
change in my attitude toward this grim
hostelry of pain. It seemed no longer quite so
forbidding: I was not alien, I was initiate,
sealed to the order by suffering. It was not that
I liked it better, but that I had begun, curiously,
to feel myself a part of it, constrained to share
its fortunes, whatever they might be. One night,
I recall vividly awakening in the warm dark-
ness, looking at the dim light on the narrow
wall, listening to the wind that crept and called
and whistled at my window—for it was now
the dead of winter. I had suddenly the feeling
that I was in the cabin of some great ship. It

was like a great ship; and I outward bound, with a thousand other souls, for some far port. Were we safe? Were we safe?

Outside I could hear feet pacing the muffled deck and from time to time the signal that called the captain to some part of the great ship. The orderlies, they would be the stewards, and the nurses, the stewardesses: and there were the robust young officers who came to reassure the suffering or fearful passengers. There on the stand by my side stood the veritable flowers my friends had brought, a *bon voyage* for my journey.

It was an idea that grew upon my imagination. After I had recovered sufficiently to be wrapped up in warm blankets it was down the gangway they trundled me, and I was placed in a steamer chair on the lee deck. Even the incongruity of snow on the ground, the roar in the streets, the sun gleaming palely through the murk of the city, and a sparrow perched on the rail, did not shake my feeling that it was a ship I was travelling in.

There is loneliness on a long voyage, even to

one who has learned in some measure to live in the house of his own spirit—and one turns with eagerness to his fellow passengers. Strange men and women whom he has never seen before, nor heard of, and yet they are somehow bound to him and he to them by the common experiences and dangers of the voyage. Who are they, then? What is their port? It is like that greater and sometimes painful voyage on the good ship Earth, where, whether we like it or not, we are fellow passengers with many a strange human being.

It is singular, in a ship, how much one can come to know of his fellow voyagers by mere propinquity, by chance meetings on the deck, by random talk in the saloons. When one hears a man groaning piteously in an adjoining cabin, how can he avoid coming presently to know something about him? Without ever having seen him I came to know quite well a fine young officer who had had his leg amputated three times and was tossing in a wild delirium of fever. How I watched for news of his progress as it came daily by way of the attendants; and what relief when at length he won the doubtful struggle! I had been easily comfortable, I thought, compared with him.

"When you go out," I said one day to my nurse, "set the screen a little aside so that I can look through the door."

With my head properly bolstered up I watched the people going by in the broad corridor, and it made me think of the road in my own town, and all the curious people that ride or drive or walk in it. And many of them I thought I should like well if I could come to know them better. One in particular I watched for every day, a blind man, walking quickly, chin up, a woman, I thought a nurse, guiding him, with her arm locked firmly through his. Blind he was, and yet there was something confident and courageous about him. Possibly, I thought, he is going on to the eye clinic: he is bracing himself for an operation.

"Who is the blind man who goes by every day?" I asked finally.

"Why, that," replied my nurse, "is Dr. ——,

and that is not a nurse but his wife who guides him."

"A doctor!"

"Yes, Dr. ——."

Something, a very little, I uncurled of his story: the courage of it, the toil of it, the devotion of it—and indeed the success of it. He might well have excused himself in facing life —"Doth God exact day-labour, light deny'd?" —but he had gone onward, centring all the powers that remained to him in the touch of his strong and delicate fingers. He had found a calling fitted to his gifts. He was a kind of sculptor in living tissues, nerves, bones. A story one liked to enlarge upon: to tell himself!

As I began to creep out in my long gown, like some preposterously old man, I could look in as I passed at many a half-screened doorway. If one could but capture it, I thought, there was a story in every room. Not petty stories either, dealing with inconsequential things, but going down deep where life turns upon the stark realities of pain and sorrow and death. I came during the days of my slow recovery to know

a little of some of them. One of the voyagers
was a mere lad, suffering the aftermath of
infantile paralysis, lying with his legs painfully
strapped and weighted. He had been on a long,
long voyage, and upon reaching port he would
probably have to limp ashore: and yet a cheerier
lad I never saw—the slow Southern humour in
the turn of his voice, the glint in his eye. I liked
to have him wheeled into my room for a visit—
he in his chair and I in my bed. No lugubrious
conversation did we indulge in, never a word of
commiseration, but gusts of laughter that there
should be so many ridiculous and humorous
things in a hospital.

One passenger I came to know had been long
on his voyage: a seasoned traveller compared
with me. He had many books on his cabinet,
symbols of his permanence, and framed pictures
near him on his stand, one of a splendid boy
who was, I learned, his son. He read me a poem
he had written—"in the nights when I find it
hard to sleep"—and it was for this son he wrote
it. The refrain alone I recall because it contained, bound up in a few words, what he him-

self had learned during his hard voyage. This
was it:

Plough on, my son, plough on.

Another man I chanced to meet during these
days of my own slow recovery had an indescribable fascination for me. *He was going to die
and did not know it.* Everyone about seemed
aware of it. It was the bandied news of the corridor. A significant look of the eye, a nod of the
head as one went by his door—there in that
room is a man who is going to die.

It gave me the strangest sense of tense aware-
ness. I had, in the past, seen men die; I had
known the sorrow of the death of dear friends;
but death—it is curious when I think of it—
had never for me, previous to my experience in
the hospital, seemed at all a reality. It was something terrible that happened to other people, and
though it may appear shocking in the telling,
but it is so, I thought of it somehow as their
own fault. Here it had come close to me in many
forms as a stark reality: something that might
even happen to *me*. In this place it was no longer

a phenomenon, but a measurable and daily expectancy. It was this new congeries of observation and intense feeling that so stirred my interest in this man who was going to die—and did not know it!

One day I met him. He had read something I had once written and asked if I would come to see him. I went with the greatest hesitation and reluctance, and yet with an overpowering curiosity. How must a man feel who was about to die? What would he think? How would he look? What would he say? As I walked down the corridor with the nurse who brought the message, these questions came upon me with a vividness and power I cannot describe. In my imagination I saw the poor fellow in bed, emaciated, slow of breath, feebly reaching out his hand to touch mine. I could scarcely control the beating of my heart or the trembling of my knees when I stepped around the screen.

"How are you, sir?" said a steady voice. "Come in. I'm glad to see you."

There he sat in his chair, a stout, rather florid man, in a gay-coloured dressing gown. There were flowers on his table—a world of flowers —and pictures of a smiling gray-haired woman and a smiling girl and two little boys. In front of him, on a desk, piles of neatly arranged papers, as though he had just looked up from his daily affairs. It was I who was hesitant and embarrassed: for I could not quickly adjust reality and preconception. It was he who made everything easy and hospitable.

While I sat talking with him a nurse brought in a telegram, which he slit open in the quick, nervous, incidental manner of the business man. He glanced at it and tossed it on the desk, proceeding with his conversation.

It came over me with a kind of shock. What futile urgency—if the man was going to die. Then I remembered, with a wave of pity, that he did not know!

It was not long before I could place him. He was quite a typical American business man— self-confident, positive, vital. He did not tell me in so many words that he was rich: he radiated it. He told me of a "deal" he had just "cleared up" in which he had made a "killing." I found that his secretary came in every morning to take care of "a lot of little matters."

I kept forgetting—but it would come over me suddenly and with a sinking sense of futility, "Why all these deals? What good making any more money? The man is going to die."

The next day when I stopped to see him I found the nurse reading a newspaper aloud, and when he began to talk of the depression in business and the outlook for certain stocks, I kept saying to myself, "Now, what is the use of all that?"

He talked again quite volubly about himself and his affairs: but presently he broke off, and I saw him looking at me with a slow, inscrutable gaze.

"Are you here for long?" he asked.

As I paused I thought his look intensified, and there was something deep down and far back in his narrowing eyes—or did I imagine it?—that was pitiful to see.

"The doctors," said I, "are promising me that I can go home for Christmas."

I shall never forget the pause that followed

—my glance drifted away to the picture of the smiling gray-haired woman on his table—nor the peculiar tone of his voice—deep, still—one word:

"Christmas!"

They had all said he did not know, but I knew as well as though he had told me in so many words. He knew! No doubt he had known all along! My whole heart went out to him so that I could scarcely keep the tears from my eyes. I looked at him again. Yes, there was a kind of mediocrity about the man, he had few intellectual resources, but what a fighter! What a fighter! He was playing the game straight through to the end. It seemed to me at the moment as though, of all things in the world, such courage, such steadiness, was most to be admired. He had not thought out a philosophy: he *had it*. He could walk up to death with it.

Telegrams, yes, why not? Deals, yes, why not? A secretary every morning to take his letters, why not? They were not futilities, they were of the essence of the matter. He was refusing to be beaten by the past or crushed by the future. He was living, as a man ought to live, every fibre of him, in the only moment he ever really possesses—this moment! It came to me with intolerable clarity: "Why, we're all going to die and don't know it; and this is what we should do about it."

I cannot tell what the man's religious beliefs were—if he had any. Once or twice during the few days I knew him he seemed on the point of saying something to me—I knew!—but the moment passed. How I should have liked to know! But of this I am certain: he had faith— faith of some kind. Men differ in that: I have mine and you yours. In its essence it is a deep, deep sense of confidence—of calmness—that whatever happens, whatever the process, it is natural, it is universal, it is according to law.

I saw, borne down the long corridor, a still, white-covered figure quite cured of the fever of living.

"To die is different from what anyone supposed—and luckier."

XI LIFE AND THE DOCTOR

XI

LIFE AND THE DOCTOR

I will make a man more precious than fine gold.

MY HOSPITAL grew on me as I came to know it better. Everything in it and about it began to interest me profoundly. I learned through books and in bits of conversation the story of the man who gave the money to found it. His portrait hangs there in the anteroom, a bluff business man, one of those Americans who insisted upon his practicality, and wrote his poetry in brick and mortar. At the main entrance to the vast building there stands, without warning or explanation, a colossal statue of the Christ, his hands outspread in welcome. Strange in that busy place: a personality as disturbing as ever to the spirit

of man. On the pedestal these words are en-
graved:

Come unto me all ye that labour and are heavy laden
and I will give you rest.

I liked to watch the busy crowds swirling by
in the passageways, pale new patients coming
in, smiling patients going out, visitors to see the
sick, hurrying doctors and nurses—few looking
up as they went by. I thought of another line
that might well be placed upon the pedestal: "Is
it nothing to you, all ye that pass by?"

There were also the great doctors—the great
men—who created the living hospital within
its shell of brick and mortar, and by their genius
made it famous. I had their books, one by one,
and read deeply into their hopes and their
aspirations, felt their passion for truth, was convinced by their practical sense. I was full of
admiration. One of the greatest of them knew
as much of the human spirit as of the human
body.

It seemed to me, indeed, the more I saw, and
learned, and felt, that of all institutions in this

world, the hospital, at this moment of time, is supreme. It represents modern man at his best. It is the most objective and dispassionate in confronting the problems of life, the least controlled by prejudices or traditions or taboos. As I thought of it, it seemed to me far more vitally in contact with reality, more definite in its purpose, and therefore more effective as an institution, than the church, the school, the senate.

Here, I thought, a man's a man for a' that. He is accepted without regard to class, or race, or creed, or sex. In the ward where I lay, during many weeks of my sojourn, I had for neighbours a justice of the United States Supreme Court, a United States Senator, the president-elect of a Latin American republic, and a miscellaneous assortment of the rich and notable of the earth—all looking much alike in their hospital slips. Down the corridor a little way there opened the vast wards where lay the utterly poor and neglected of that city—the poorest white people, the poorest foreigners, the poorest Negroes. So far as the essentials of medical attention were concerned, they enjoyed exactly the same treatment as the Senators and the millionaires. A little less room, perhaps, in the public wards, and simpler food, but the same exactitude of scientific care by doctors and nurses. A black-hearted criminal, if he comes to the hospital shot through, is cared for and cured; he has the same attention as a saint might have—and no questions asked about either.

After I was able to make little venturesome excursions through the mazes of that endless institution, I walked one evening into the Negro ward. Every bed was filled; everywhere I looked there were cleanliness and order, and busy nurses and doctors. Some of these poor of the earth, even though ill, were probably warmer, cleaner, better fed, more comfortably housed than ever before in their lives. It was just at their supper time, and the orderlies were trundling in the steaming service tables. One old coloured man with kinky gray hair, propped up in his bed, eating his supper, looked so happy that I spoke to him.

"Dese folks," he responded, "am sholy de messengers ob de Lawd."

A little later, coming back slowly along the corridor, I heard sounds strange in that place. I stopped at the entrance of the passageway that led down into the Negro ward. They had finished their supper and had broken irresistibly into song. This was the refrain:

> "Oh, I know, I know
> The Lawd has laid his hands on me."

Standing there, listening, I could not keep the mist out of my eyes.

Yes, the colour of men still divides them, and their religions divide them, and their languages and their nations and their parties, but this great ship of souls accepts them all, carries them all onward together to their destination, steerage, third class, and first! Only one question is asked of any man: "Do you suffer?" We are all one in pain!

If it was the conviction of the preciousness of the soul of man that built the cathedral at Chartres, it is the conviction of the preciousness

of his life that has built the matchless hospitals
of America. As I thought of it, those long days,
it seemed to me that the hospital cherishes a
spirit, or an attitude, that the Church sadly
lacks. I felt in it a respect for the human body
and for human life beyond that in the Church,
as it stands to-day, for the spirit of man. The
hospital diagnoses before it prescribes; the
Church prescribes before it diagnoses. The
physician stands humble before the human
body, studies it, doubts about it, wonders at it;
labours to fit his remedies to the exact disease.
Is there in any church an equivalent humility
in the presence of the spirit of man? Is the
priest willing to inquire and doubt and wonder?
Does he *know* before he tries to cure? Must the
Church cultivate certainty lest knowledge turn
and rend it?

Once the physician let blood indiscriminately
for almost every ill. Has the Church in its treatment of souls passed that stage in its develop-
ment? And where, in any religious institution,
is there such singleness of purpose, such objec-
tivity of aim, as in the hospital?

And yet, having said all these things about the hospital, and truly said, for they are based upon what I myself saw and heard and thought, I have yet to speak of a limitation I felt deeply during the weeks I spent there. One of the vivid lesser characters that Shakespeare drew with such penetrating art was a doctor. I thought often, while in the hospital, of that nameless doctor in *Macbeth*. It is after the murder, and Lady Macbeth walks in her restless sleep. The doctor comes in, comes bustling in, all doctor, inquiring of the nurse:

"When was it she last walked?"

He is eager for all the facts before he makes his diagnosis. And then, you will remember, Lady Macbeth enters—in that scene that freezes the blood. She is washing her hands.

"Out, damned spot! out, I say . . . all the perfumes of Arabia will not sweeten this little hand. Oh, oh, oh!"

Faced with this appalling spectacle, the boundless agony of the soul, the doctor rises suddenly out of his profession, realizes that here are matters too great for him.

"This disease," he says, "is beyond my practice."

He watches the rising terror of the distraught Queen: "There's knocking at the gate": and out of his deep understanding as a man, he says:

"More needs she the divine than the physician."

It seemed to me—I may be wrong—that it is too rarely that the modern doctor, equipped with his myriad instruments, is willing to say, "This disease is beyond my practice," and more rarely still, "More needs she the divine than the physician."

When I thought, after eight doctors had weighed and tested and X-rayed every part of me, how little, after all, they knew of *me,* it came to me with extraordinary force, the vast ranges of human suffering, suffering that reacts upon the body, that is beyond the practice of the doctor. They try, humbly enough, to get inside the mind of the patient, but something fails in their art; something else is needed; some deeper, humbler understanding of the human spirit. There are such depths of human life that the photograph never catches! Nearly all that is important or uniquely interesting about man begins, as Matthew Arnold once said, where nature ends. It is relatively easy to observe and explain and treat the physical reactions of humankind, for they are the common reactions of all animals and make up indeed a large part of life: but it is the plane that lies above all this, however profoundly affected by it, that so intensely matters. We are all alike as animals: we are all different as human beings. In the slight margin by which man lifts his head above the universal slime and *thinks,* lies all the interest and beauty of life, likewise all the tragedy and sorrow—and joy.

What it seemed to me I wanted, passionately, in that hospital, was not merely a cure for my defective body, but a way to live with tranquillity in a troubled world of which my body was the apt symbol. And where is that to be had in all its vast array of medical lore, or among its most skilful physicians?

All my meditations brought me back inevitably

to the conclusion of the early weeks in the gabled room. A man after all cures himself! It is only as he comes to his own aid, takes possession of his own spirit, that he "recovers."

"To-day I have got out of all trouble or rather I have cast out all trouble, for it was not outside, but within."

As I look back upon it, I can say honestly that my experience in the hospital, miserable as it seemed at the time, was among the most interesting of my life.

XII CONVALESCENCE: "PLEASE YOU, DRAW NEAR"

XII

CONVALESCENCE: "PLEASE YOU, DRAW NEAR"

. . . that serene and blessed mood
In which . . . we are laid asleep
In body, and become a living soul.

I SHALL never forget the still routine of
the days of my slow convalescence, especially
the unhurried ease and silence of the long evenings after the day nurse had gone home and I
lay propped up in my bed with a light over my
shoulder and a priceless book on the corner of
the near-by table. What peace, what ease, what
comfort, now that the ordeal was over. While
I was sometimes in pain and often restless and
uncomfortable—and weak, weak!—yet there
was an indescribable sense of renewed security,
a wayward freedom of the mind, I had not
known before in years I dare not count.

All my life, it seemed to me, I had been hard

driven, often forced to tasks that were not
easily native to my gifts, that which was most
myself interrupted and retarded by a thousand dusty, inconsequential affairs. Temptations
to go here or hurry there, see this or hear that,
by some stupid outward urge. All the compul-
sions of loyalty and duty! Even in my own little
place there had seemed literally a conspiracy
against quietude and thought, against the deep
examination of life, against such small effort
as a man may make to understand the world
which surrounds and so ruthlessly compels him.

But here, what unspeakable luxury! No
sense of being driven either by outward or inward taskmasters, no duties, no engagements,
no interruptions. None of the absurd compul-
sions of property or the urgings of ambition or
the weariness of routine. All day long one can
lie or sit still, save for the fortunate moments
when the nurse comes in smiling with the tray,
or in the evening after a tap on one's door, with
the prescribed "nourishment," which proves to
be a glass of iced orange juice beaten foamy
with the white of an egg—wholly delicious. The

world has slipped away from us, and we do
not care! So much that had seemed wayward
becomes wisdom and joy. I wonder if there is
anything in this world comparable to the sense
of being fully alive within—warm and strong
there, eager there! I shall never forget the re-
curring sense I had that whatever I may have
lost in time or strength or money I had regained
in self-possession. I was at liberty to think anything I liked, go anywhere I pleased, past,
present, or future—I was free to see or hear or
feel whatsoever I would or could. Here no one
kept a clock on me! Not even that most arbi-
trary of clock keepers, myself. I could take up
any book I liked—for I was as long-armed as
the resources of that great hospital—and if I
did not like it, I could put it down. I could write
one sentence in my familiar book, or ten or
twenty, or none at all, as I pleased, or I could
turn to the wall (the nurse thinking I slept)
and listen to the December rain drumming on
the window, and let my mind go free among
what William James calls "the deepest things
of our nature . . . the dumb regions of the

heart in which we dwell alone with our willing-
nesses and unwillingnesses, our faiths and our
fears."

Many times in my life I have repeated Rodin's
saying, a true maxim for every craftsman, that
"slowness is beauty"—but until those days in
the hospital I never knew fully what it meant.
To read slowly, to think slowly, to feel slowly
and deeply: what enrichment! In the past I have
been so often greedy. I have gobbled down innumerable facts, ideas, stories, poetical illusions
—I have gobbled down work—I have even
gobbled down my friends!—and indeed had a
kind of enjoyment of all of them—but rarely
have I tasted the last flavour of anything, the
final exquisite sense of personality or spirit that
secretes itself in every work that merits serious
attention, in every human being at all worth
knowing. But in those heavenly evenings of
silence and solitude I read only a little at a time
and only the greatest books, especially those
great-small books in which some master spirit
has completely delivered himself. I read until
I came upon something that stirred me deep

down, something strong and hard, something a little difficult, at first, to understand, and there I stopped and slowly, slowly, turned it over in my mind until I knew exactly what it was the prophet or the poet or the philosopher was trying to say to me. And always, I found, the subtlest beauties, the deepest truths, came last.

In one of Dr. Osler's provocative addresses, for example, I found a reference to a passage in Sir Thomas Browne which he himself had loved. So I got me the *Urn-Burial* and the *Religio Medici* to find it, and read all around and about it, and wore it afterwards for many a day like a jewel in my mind—and love it yet!

". . . the iniquity of oblivion blindly scattereth her poppy and deals with the memory of man without regard to merit of perpetuity."

Writers have taken whole pages to say less!

Often I found passages, especially in the old books, that seemed, as the Quakers say, to speak to my condition, and these I sometimes committed to memory that I might have them ready, loaded weapons, when skulking pain attacked me or mutinous dullness threatened to wear me down.

"I affirm that tranquillity is nothing else than the good ordering of the mind. Constantly then give to thyself this retreat and renew thyself; and let thy principles be brief and fundamental, which, as soon as thou shalt recur to them, will be sufficient to cleanse the soul completely and to send thee back free from all discontent with the things to which thou returnest."

A page of Marcus Aurelius, indeed, is worth, any time, a day's slowness. What fortification of the spirit! What incentives to courage! Open anywhere, at random, and feel the keen, bracing, sometimes scarifying, truth.

"I have often wondered how it is that every man loves himself more than all the rest of men, but yet sets less value on his own opinion of himself than on the opinion of others."

Or of death:

"Thou hast embarked, thou hast made the voyage, thou art come to shore; get out."

Many and rich treasures were thus available in the days of my convalescence that I should

have felt it impossible in my busy, ordinary life
to enjoy. I thought often what a perfect thing
it was to have all about me for days at a time
such a variety of fine thoughts, plucked in pass-
ing out of old books like scented flowers from
half-forgotten roadsides. I thought also that if
I were again in my customary life I should not
only lack the time, but possibly also the courage,
to be going about wearing such ornaments—at
least in a conspicuous buttonhole. What
cowards we are, anyway! What Peters warm-
ing ourselves at the fire, denying that we know
anything that is great or true or beautiful! How
rarely we dare let anyone see our best possessions—the things we really live by—lest they
fling names at us. I resolved, those days, never
any more to hurry, never to appear what I was
not, never to be constrained by the crowd. Ah,
well. . . .

It was in this time of returning zest that I
had the good fortune to read, or gloriously reread, a book that exactly fitted and interpreted
my mood. It is not often—not once a year—not
once in a lifetime, possibly—that one stumbles

upon a book that perfectly and completely
satisfies what he has at the moment burning in
his mind. I shall never forget the long, still
evening in the hospital when I read *The
Tempest*—or how I turned from it late in the
night with that sense of happiness and courage
which only the greatest art can give to the spirit
of man, saying over and over to myself those
last words of Prospero, the ripe essence of his
long experience:

"Please you, draw near."

It came to me then, as a kind of inspiration,
that better than any other words I know, they
express the final wisdom of men—men who live
in a world, not perfect, but *human*.

"Please you, draw near."

What else is it that we desire after being
buffeted by rude events, after being cast away
on our own particular desert isle, after at last
subduing our Caliban and setting free our
Ariel, save to turn with a new and deep kind
of passion to "beauteous mankind," the "goodly
creatures" all about us, and there, having be-

come quiet within ourselves, saying with deep
sincerity:

"Please you, draw near."

I have put down these incidents and thoughts
of my convalescence just as they came to me.
A certain exuberance of joyful relief is perhaps
permissible after months of anxiety and discomfort. I make no excuse for it: I have rarely
enjoyed anything more.

XIII   LETTERS DURING ILLNESS

XIII
LETTERS DURING ILLNESS

A man's life of any worth is a continual Allegory, and very
few eyes can see the Mystery of his life. . . .
From a letter by JOHN KEATS.

I NEVER before prized letters as I did during those long weeks in bed: nor read them oftener, for I learned that there is much more to be had out of even brief and simple letters, if one reads *into* them as well as *out* of them, than I had ever before imagined. They are like any other expression of friendship: we get in proportion as we give.

Harriet's letters were best, Harriet's letters, with their flowing details, the unhurried, precious reassurances of the continuity and usualness of life. I had a curious sense, in reading them, of life flowing in tranquillity: all the small ordinary daily happenings, the seasons going round, autumn deepening into winter. I felt somehow drawn into the placid regularity of nature. And they nearly always set me smiling—as though I were at home—and well again! When they came I liked to hold them in my hand for some time and then to read them slowly.

"Mrs. Sargent's daughter—you remember little Inez Sargent—has twins."

So, said I to myself, little Inez Sargent has twins. I could remember only vaguely that there was such a person as Inez Sargent, and twins are not a seventh-day marvel in the world, but somehow it was pleasing and interesting to know that little Inez Sargent had twins. Why shouldn't she have twins?

"John Heathcote has sold his Alderney cow."

How that little item brought back the veritable picture of John, his jolly old wife in the doorway, and the ancient wagon standing there by the barn, and the chickens scratching in the sunny yard. John became so fond of his horses, his cow, his pigs, that it was news indeed to hear that he had sold any of them. There is a story we delight to tell one another regarding John's sale of another cow. The purchaser was shrewd and cold-eyed and insisted on knowing how well bred the cow was and how much milk she gave. Old John looked at her with affection and responded earnestly:

"She's a good cow and gives all the milk she possibly can."

Then there were always the beguiling references to garden or orchard or meadow.

"I had Frank over to put your bees in the winter boxes."

My bees! As I lay there in bed I could follow out in my imagination every step in the process I had so often performed myself: bringing the cases out of the storehouse, setting them up on blocks of wood, lifting the hives one after another and fitting them in place, afterwards packing them carefully around with shavings. What a beautiful process!

In the future, when friends of mine are ill, I shall know well the kind of letters that will rest them most: letters full of the healthy continuity of life—letters without commiseration.

Before I was well enough to write letters myself, save a few scrawling sentences, I could at least *think* letters. I could lie perfectly still and work out the most beautiful long letters, not only to friends who were near to me, but to old friends whom I had not seen for years. Presently, having written a letter I especially enjoyed to L—— I began to consider what he might reply to me, and I soon found myself answering my own letters. Oh, I was greedy for letters! It proved delightful and cheering to put myself in the place of various friends and to write as I thought they would write. It was surprising to me how vividly it brought them back to me: let me into their lives—as I, at least, imagined them to be.

I filled many hard half hours with these pleasant excursions. When they began, a little, to pall upon me, for it was, after all, only a game, it occurred to me suddenly, and with the delight which comes with an inventive idea, that I was by no means confined, in my imaginary correspondence, to friends I knew. I had all the world to pick from! So I wrote immediately to President Hoover and received in reply—that very day!—the most amazingly confidential letter regarding his life in the White House and his real opinion of various public men—including Senator Borah! I had no end of amusement out of this for a day or so, since his letter contained the most astonishing and unbelievable revelations. If I were to disclose it to the public, it would undoubtedly cause an explosion. So I shall preserve the amenities and keep the letter to myself.

I wrote to Mussolini, dictator of Italy. Our letters were couched in severely formal language, beginning, "Sir," and ending "I am, Sir, Your obedient servant." Never before in my life have I delighted in such beautifully elaborate ironies or invented icier rejoinders—for I don't like Mussolini. I give it as my unprejudiced judgment, since I was the author of all of them, that my letters to him were far superior to his letters to me.

But the most amusing of all was the letter I

received from John D. Rockefeller, enclosing a new dime. I responded at once, in the most courteous manner, telling him in detail of all the ways in which I had considered expending his munificent gift. The more I wrote the more amusing the idea became, so that I must have laughed out loud. What a reckless spendthrift I was becoming! My nurse, who had thought me peacefully asleep in accordance with the doctor's orders, was at once aroused.

"What are you laughing at?" she asked.

"I was considering," said I, "how I would spend a new dime—if John D. Rockefeller should send me one."

I could see her face grow round with astonishment, which delighted me.

"Well, I never!" said my nurse.

I wonder if anyone has ever written such a letter to John D. Rockefeller. I think it might amuse him. Maybe I will post mine and see if he won't send me another dime.

These may seem ridiculous diversions, but they filled parts of many restless nights.

XIV. THE RETURN

XIV
THE RETURN

Henceforth I ask not good-fortune—I myself am good-fortune,
Henceforth I whimper no more, postpone no more, need nothing.

AFTER a long illness, one's recovery comes
like the spring in our Northern valleys. It
was in late April I came home again. Days
there were, the foredawn of the year, days of
such magical sweetness and warmth that it
seemed of a certainty spring had come. New
soft foliage on the poplars, the golden mists of
the elm trees, hyacinths under the sumacs!
One's mind runs away toward recovery far
faster than his body.

Then come days of sad withdrawal, days of
cloudy hesitation when the budding year retires
within a gray cowl of penitence. We have cold

rains slanting down, flurries of reminiscent snow, piercing winds out of the northwest, and all the world again turns chill and drab.

One does not, fortunately, know it at the time, but there are two periods of convalescence. I think I have not spoken too ardently of the first, with its joyous sense of renewed security. I found the second, after my return, more difficult to bear, in certain ways, than the early days of my illness when pain and discomfort were expected and studied occupations. I, too, had my cold rains slanting down, I had my cowl of penitence. Heavy weeks of slow recovery there were, when every instinct of my nature cried out for rest. Stop! Wait! Any road I walked grew intolerably long; any hill I climbed, too high; all the work I did, too hard. Such an appetite for recovery, so little food to satisfy it!

In the hospital, during my convalescence, I had no need of any outward action or responsibility; I could devote my entire attention to delightful excursions in the quiet and happy country of the mind. I had now to take myself over, a going concern, and try to catch step with a swift-moving and clamorous world. Those who have themselves been ill will know well the feeling of that time, and the discouragements of it.

What a blessing, those days, I found in my garden and orchard, and especially among my bees. I shall not easily forget the spacious quietude of those May mornings, with the sun looking in over the hills of Pelham, and the dew still on the grass, the meadows green again, and the apple trees beginning to bloom.

I know of nothing that will more completely absorb the mind than the slow, careful, minute tasks of the bee master. Other familiar labour of the garden or farm or orchard, for want of variety, sometimes loses its charm, but one may find an inexhaustible delight in the strange ways of the bee people. After many years' experience I am as much interested as ever I was. I am still a besotted amateur!

In the hard days of my convalescence I found nothing that fitted so exactly the limitations of my physical strength and at the same time satisfied the appetite aroused during my illness for that which was slow and deep and still. One cannot force nature; a bee keeper who hurries soon repents!

How pleasant it was, then, sitting there in the scented orchard with my back to the sun, slowly going through the hives. Slowly! never making a false motion, lifting the bee-covered frames, examining the state of the brood and stores, watching for her majesty the queen, learning at a glance whether the colony has begun rearing drones, and finding and cutting out the new queen cells. A fascinating process, never more easily practised than at this season of the year when the bees are busy and comfortable with new stores of nectar and pollen coming in. One need scarcely wear a bee veil or gloves if he knows how to go about the delicate business with that courtesy and gentleness due to the manners and customs of an ancient society. When I began bee keeping, now long ago, I was often stung, but in the last half dozen years I have had scarcely a half dozen stings, and these were usually due to my own haste or stupidity. I think sometimes that almost all the mistakes I have made in my life have been the result of haste.

When I grew weary, and this at first was often enough, I stopped where I sat and watched the urgent, unself-conscious, strangely beguiling life of the world of the bee people with its unfathomable social laws and its intricate customs. I watched the workers darting out of the hive with a kind of fierce energy, lifting in the sunny air, circling once or more about, and then with swift certainty heading for the blossom fields where their harvest was making. I watched them coming in again heavily laden with pollen and nectar, often so weary with their load that they could not quite make the landing board, waddling into the hive like tipsy sailors with their dunnage bags full of yellow or brown or red pollen. I watched the young bees coming out when the sun grew warm and the air dry to play in front of the hive, using their new wings with inimitable grace, preparing themselves for the stern labour soon to come.

It is a beautiful process and grows upon one

as he becomes intimately familiar with the significance of all the sights, sounds, odours of
the hive, and the varied habits of its long-settled
social life. A hard-and-fast communism if ever
there was one, with the life of the individual
wholly devoted to the welfare of the swarm!
To look down into it one feels like some god
watching for his own delight the flowing life
of a world as distant from his own, as self-
contained as it is unconscious of his existence.
He may destroy it—destruction is easy for a
god!—or he may, by acting upon laws wholly
beyond the range of the bee world, work strange
miracles with it—like putting into a colony
frames of brood or honey the bees have not
themselves made, or cutting out the queen cells,
or clipping the wings of the queen herself so
that the colony cannot swarm. He may in some
degree direct the activities of the bees so that
they serve his purposes as well as their own—
purposes of which they know nothing—but he
cannot, for all his power and his knowledge,
change in the slightest particular the ages-old
Law of the Hive. He himself, however

omniscient, can work with the colony only as he himself also learns and obeys the laws of it.

I have sometimes speculated upon what might be the thinking of a philosopher of the swarm, if such could possibly be imagined. He would be no worker—workers are too busy making and banking their honey—nor yet a queen, since the queen is absorbed in the domestic affairs of the hive. Probably an old, idling drone with little to do in the world but loaf and invite his soul: *he* would be the Philosopher! He could perhaps predicate, from the evidences of what he might call Providence or Fate or Miracle—or Law!—the existence of a Power Beyond the Hive. He might speculate as to its attributes and its purposes, marvel at its paradoxes, consider its will, but what, after all, could he know of *Me?*

Often, if I tired of working with or watching the bees, I would recall, as I sat there in the sun, some of the things that had come to my mind while I was in the hospital, especially if they seemed applicable to the moment. One passage occurred to me that I did not even know I had kept in my memory. It was from Dr. Johnson, and I have since looked it up to see that I quoted it correctly.

"No man," said he, "is obliged to do as much as he can do. A man is to have part of his life to himself."

I liked especially the last half of this quotation and said it over a number of times as I sat there, idling, by the hives: "A man is to have part of his life to himself."

Another passage I repeated upon occasions when I began to feel, in my weakness, that the world was too much for me:

". . . a man of understanding hath lost nothing, if he yet have himselfe."

But I loved most of all, in those days, to lose myself completely in the unhurried enjoyment, the concentration of the entire mind, upon the simple tasks in hand. I liked even the somewhat monotonous work of preparing new hives, stringing the brood frames with wire, and setting in the foundation comb. I liked to fit together the comb-honey sections—how good the odour of the clean new white-wood!—and wax in the starters. There is salvation alike to worn bodies and tired souls in these quiet and simple processes of the hands. The knotted strands of life are thus by slow magic untangled, and one comes to be like a child, absorbed in play, with the world grown newly happy. And it is no mere anodyne of escape, for there is in it the ancient logic of labour, wherein the result is honey in the honeycomb!

All of these experiences and meditations helped greatly during the days of what I have called my second convalescence, before I dared test my strength with any real labour. Idle days they were, lazy, still, rich days, full of a kind of delight I had never quite felt before. For I found myself willing to be slow and quiet, to look long at one thing! In the old life I was scarcely ever able to wait until the full meaning, or beauty, of anything—whether the aspects of nature or the written word—came in upon me. I was too swift: what I planted yesterday in the fertile soil of my spirit I wanted to pull up to-day to see if the roots had sprouted. I was not willing to be quiet and await the sure processes of the sun and the rain. All Americans are something like that. In our bemused faith in speed we think some instrument can be had that will obliterate time and shorten growth; but the law of the spirit is not unlike that of the body: the period of silent gestation that must follow the conception of thought is immutable.

"Those too are triflers," says the philosopher, "who have wearied themselves in life by their activity."

As I grew stronger I began to have, day by day, a keener sense of life—the *intensity* of life. Even the small and disagreeable chores of the orchard and the land became immeasurably precious to me; I even had days when I felt that I could write again. I was humbly thankful that I could do anything at all! One morning in particular I remember vividly—so vividly that I wrote down an account of the incident in my notebook under the date of May 14th—I was standing at the top of a ladder, flinging out clouds of vile-smelling sulphur and arsenate of lead. We were spraying the apple trees. Down below, Frank, my helper, was pumping the ancient contraption which we had tinkered into another year's service.

"Pump, Frank, pump for your life."

And Frank pumped, and I sent a mist of poison into the topmost branches. We had studied the light morning airs and moved slowly around each tree until every calyx had had its minute attention.

"A good job," said Frank. "I guess that'll give 'em the stomach ache."

It may seem ridiculous, for this is quite the most disagreeable task of the garden, but it suddenly came over me, as I stood perched high on the ladder, in the full glory of the morning, that there was something incalculably and indescribably beautiful about it all. I was newly and intensely aware of the robins singing, and the bees humming in the near-by hives, and the sun looking down the hill with the promise of a fair and perfect morning. I caught myself saying under my breath: "Thank God, thank God." It seemed as though, doubter as I am, that God was somewhere not distant, and easily to be thanked. I felt like pinning this date in May, as Pascal pinned the date of his conversion, to an inner garment over my heart.

As I came up the hill a little later I saw pale yellow tulips blooming among the low-growing phlox, and the wisteria on the porch, grown eager in the summery days of May, hanging full of half-opened blossoms, delicate, lacy, more like a mist of beauty than a realized blooming—I saw all these things as I never had seen or felt them before.

"Thank God," I said, "I am well again! I can work again."

XV THE PUMPKIN PIE

XV

THE PUMPKIN PIE

That which is not natural is not perfect.

IT WAS not really until autumn, a full year after I was taken ill, that I had final and convincing evidences of my recovery. To a man accustomed all his life to robust health—the health that glows with outdoor life—the loss of appetite which accompanies a long illness, though the doctors may consider it of minor importance, is nevertheless one of the major woes. For it is a fact that two of the senses which give us the most powerful grasp upon the good, homely realities of life—I mean the sense of smell and the sense of taste—lose their delight when one cannot enjoy his daily food. They told me I was convalescent long before I believed what they said. I did not go to dinner like an army with banners!

When the leaves began to turn, and the apples were ripe, and there was a frosty zest in the morning air, I began, after a long forenoon in the garden or orchard, or tramping in country roads, to be conscious that there was something in life quite worth living for. By twelve o'clock I was listening eagerly for a call from the house. And finally, one day, really for the first time, I knew I had come fully alive.

At dinner on that unforgettable occasion there appeared in all its glory the most perfect pumpkin pie that ever I saw in my life. It was like a full moon, crimped about with little flaky clouds of piecrust, and being just from the oven —I *hate* clammy pies!—it gave off the ambrosia of the gods. Nowhere else on earth, save in New England, has pumpkin pie reached the final stage of perfection: for in New England, by one of those daring incongruities or disharmonies that mark the highest art, it is often not made of pumpkin at all, but of squash.

There it was, then, reposing in all its re-

fulgence of golden glory upon our largest dinner plate. Little brown and yellow bubbles had
worked upon its surface a kind of autumnal pat-
tern, and the crinkled rim of crust about it was
exactly of the right colour to tempt the eye,
for it promised to melt in the mouth.

"A wonderful pie," said I to Harriet.

"Wait until you taste it," said she.

So she drew the knife across it and cut out
and lifted a generous slice—I give my word it
was all of two inches thick!—and having placed
it carefully upon a little plate, passed it along
to me. There it was, a deep, luscious yellow,
shading to orange, all warm and moist and rich
and full of ravishing odours.

"This surely," said I, "is one of the great
moments of life."

"Ridiculous," said Harriet, "eat it, eat it!"

"Slowly, slowly," said I, "one thing at a
time. This is no occasion for usurpation by any
one of the senses. This is not merely for tasting
but for smelling and seeing, and, I think, for
touching also——"

"Don't touch it! Eat it!"

"I expect also," said I, "if one's hearing were sufficiently acute—say as good as a honeybee's —he could also find keen enjoyment in listening to what is going on inside of this delectable pie——"

"I never saw your like," interrupted Harriet.

"All the faint little bubblings and boilings and dissolvings and settlings left over from the oven. He could see, too, if his eyes were perfect, the delicate aroma, the veritable spirit— one might call it the animate mist—rising from this pie——"

"Stop, stop!"

"As I said, the animate mist of the pie, charged with the spices of Araby, rising out of its delicious hidden recesses——"

"When *are* you going to eat that pie?"

"When I have enjoyed it sufficiently beforehand," said I to Harriet. "When I have reached the appropriate place in the ritual. Let me ask you this: is there any point in taking less enjoyment out of nature than one is capable of doing? Why walk on one leg when you have two? Or use one sense when you have five? In this degenerate and greedy age, are we grown to be savages, willing to bolt our beauty?"

"And," interposed Harriet with spirit, "philosophize until our pie is cold."

"And," continued I, "merely eat our pie?"

I found myself waving my fork in the air. The last remark of Harriet much impressed me; it was extremely sensible. So I fell to—as the unctuous older writers used to say—and without further excursions into philosophy or poetry ate every crumb of my triangle of pie.

I have thought since how I could express the sensations of that blissful moment, and have decided that language is a beggarly medium, wholly incapable, whether with adjectives, verbs, or nouns, of giving even a hazy conception of what I was experiencing. My only recourse is to ask any possible reader of these lines to think back, carefully, along the whole course of his life and recall the moment of his greatest gustatory adventure, the most poignant thrill that the art of cookery ever gave him, and let me assure him that my experience at dinner with that perfect pumpkin pie was equal to, or possibly greater than, his noblest moment.

"Well," said I, lifting at length my napkin, "this has been one of the notable incidents of my career."

"Ridiculous!" commented Harriet.

"I shall never forget it," said I. "Heaven has no greater bliss for the souls of the saved!"

With such evidences as these, how can I doubt the completeness of my recovery?

THE END